To Maria,

I hope you really enjoy this book. Good luck w/ you at Kentuck!

Ricky J William

Copyright© July 2004 Lilisa J. Williams

All rights reserved.

ISBN: 1501967010

For additional copies of this book or to arrange for a seminar by this author please contact:

Lilisa J. Williams
President and Founder
Performance Strategies Unlimited, Inc.
A Motivation, Leadership and Empowerment Training Institute
PO Box 5853
Hillside, NJ 07205
(908) 432-1853
(908) 964-4848 (fax)
www.performancestrategiesunlimited.net
info@performancestrategiesunlimited.net

Release Your Power

Edited by: Kara Ann Suttora
Printed by: Instant Publisher
Published by: Anointed 4 Production
                  PO Box 5853
                  Hillside, NJ 07205

Release Your Power

"Eight Strategies for Becoming Who You Really Are"

Lilisa J. Williams

And Stephen, full of faith and power,
did great wonders and miracles
among the people.
ACTS 6:8

The power in which we must have faith
if we would be well, is the creative and
curative power which exists in every
living thing.
JOHN HARVEY KELLOGG

For the kingdom of God is not in word,
but in power.
I CORINTHIANS 4:20

We are not human beings
having a spiritual experience.
We are spiritual beings having
a human experience.
TEILHARD DE CHARDIN

Acknowledgements

To my seven siblings:

Beverly K. Carter

> For being a support and for rendering steadfast love and honesty when I needed it most. Thanks for helping to save my life.

Holly A. Kelly

> For your persistence in telling me that this project would be completed once I got started and stuck to it.

Hope L. Johnson

> For teaching me to always keep it real!

Jan L. Muhammad

> For showing me your creative side and encouraging me that I had one too. Thank you for being the example that anything can be done once we put our mind to it.

Eric C. Robinson

> For teaching me what brotherhood is truly about. Thanks for not being afraid to be smart.

Steve E. Robinson

> For being a protection for me whenever needed as we were growing up. Thanks for fighting for me until I learned to fight for myself. Thanks for teaching me how to "not cry over spilled milk."

Jesus Christ

> For setting me free, opening my eyes, healing me, saving me, leading me to all peace and joy and so much more.

Thanks to each of you for helping me to be who I really am. A special thanks to all my sisters for allowing me to be the mother that I never was.

This book is Dedicated to....

My Heavenly Father, God
My Lord and Savior, Jesus Christ
My Comforter, Holy Spirit

The Late Lillian B. Little *My Beloved Grand-mother*
Drew T. Williams *My Husband*
Pastor Barbara Branson *My Mother*
The Late Rev. Jesse Robinson Jr. *My Father*
The Late Tina Williams *My Mother In Law*
The Late Andrew Williams *My Father In Law*
The Late Jesse Robinson Sr. *My Grandfather*
The Late Alex Little *My Beloved Grandfather*

For their love, inspiration and support on this project and throughout my life.

Table of Contents

Introduction... **9**

Chapter One
        Choosing to Change................................ **17**

Chapter Two
        Spending Time with YourSelf.............…… **49**

Chapter Three
        Writing it Down.. **63**

Chapter Four
        Positively Speaking................................ **71**

Chapter Five
        Making Each Step Solid........................… **79**

Chapter Six
        Building Solid Relationships....................... **87**

Chapter Seven
        Developing the Leader Within ....… **95**

Chapter Eight
        Continuous Improvement **107**

Appendix..…... *114*

Introduction

*"**A**long the road to success I discovered that I had everything I needed to succeed.* **"**

Everything I am I have always been! At least I have always had the potential to be. If I am a writer today, it is because I was a writer 47 years ago. If I am a great wife today, it is because I was a great wife 47 years ago. If I am a scholastic achiever today, it is because I have always been a scholastic achiever! The difference is, that I did not always know how to release the power to become who I really am. Today I know! From the day that I understood this truth (approximately 3 months ago) I have been on a mission to be all that I was created to be and then some. Once you know who you really are it does not take long to change into the true you.

You will be satisfied and successful when you discover the talents and gifts that have been given to you to become who you really are. The way you get to discover more talents and gifts is to fully used the ones that you already know that you have. The way to lose what you have and prevent you from getting more is to ignore (not use, not recognize) what you have already. I no longer waste time trying to figure out why I went all those years without knowing who I really was, I just focus on becoming everything that I am.

I did not become who I was created to be until the Power was Released in my life to show me who I already am. Then I realized that I had spent my entire life becoming who I AM! When you Release Your Power you will see just who you really are.

9

When I look back over my life, its like looking down a dark, dry and broken road. There where so many twists, turns and pitfalls, I did not think that I would ever end up on a smooth road. From the time I was a young girl I have faced just about every obstacle a woman, or any person for that matter, can face in life. I am all too familiar with childhood sexual abuse, rejection, low self-esteem, emotional and physical abuse, poverty and illiteracy, to name just a few. You name it, I've dealt with it. What I did not know then is that the Power to overcome everything that happened to me was within me all along. The very person that I was destined to be was with me all my life. Like me, your success is right under your nose!

Today I live to free others from the things that had me bound. I am writing this book to unequivocally let others know that - - - "where you start in life does not have to determine where you end up!" You may have started in poverty, but you can end up rich! I did! Prior to my finding my divine purpose in life, I was on a   downward spiral. That spiral started from the time I was a child and did not end until I reached my mid-40's.   It included everything from dropping out of high school at age 16 to leaving my nine year secure marriage at age 43.

Oh, there were brief moments in between when it seemed that I was getting ahead, but there was always something that would drag me back down. As far back as I can remember, I had been used, abused or confused. I always felt like a "no-body." You know, nobody that was ever going to do anything great. Nobody that would ever fulfill a purpose that was positive. Nobody that would ever be able to motivate and empower others to find and live their purpose in life. If you are reading this book then you are my credential that I am living out my life's divine purpose.

Today, my life's purpose is to teach and show others how they can live their dreams and fulfill the perfect will of God for their lives.

I cannot and will not take credit for anything that has happened in my life that is good. I know who has worked all my situations, trials and circumstances together for my good. God has done this and it is marvelous in my eyes and He and He alone gets all the Glory for my success and the things that I am able to do through Jesus Christ.

I am not afraid to say that Jesus is my source and strength in all! After having gone through what I have been through I am *__fully persuaded__* about how I made it this far. Through Christ Jesus, I learned everything I needed to know to change my life! I can truly say that "God has given me one idea that has made me rich!" I heard Dr. Creflo Dollar, the great minister from Atlanta, Georgia, say that about a year ago, and I immediately adopted it for my life. If I were you, I wouldn't waste anymore time feeling like a failure. You are not a failure! You may have failed at some things, maybe many things, but YOU ARE NOT A FAILURE.

Changing how you react to the things that happen to you can change your life for good. I have found that the critical portion of what happens to us, is not as bad as our REACTIONS to the thing that happened. Stop— — think for a minute, what would your life be like if you forgave everyone that hurts you within 2 seconds? I'll tell you, you will be living beyond your wildest dreams. Let me remind you of one true fact - - - un-forgiveness is the number one blockage to individual success.

By changing the way in which you deal with the things that happen, be it situations, setbacks and other circumstances, you can begin to change the overall impact it will have on your life. Using the processes outlined in the book, and, taking time into consideration, you too can have success by Releasing Your Power!

My mission for this book is that it will provide you with fundamental, yet basic, principles that work to establish a foundation on which to build or fortify your journey. They are practical in that you need to practice them everyday. They are foundational in that you will build on them.

Not to worry, the things are very simple. The vision must be simple, clear and plain so that you will be able to follow it without thinking hard. Some believe that it must be complicated in order for it to have real value. This might be true for some things in life. But to live a truly empowered life, you only need to follow a few basic principles and everything else will stem from there. These basic strategies are the chapter topics of this book. No doubt you already know these since they are so basic. Maybe hearing them once more will convince you that they really do work. However, they will only work if you work them. No solution, great or simple will ever work if you do not practice it regularly, consistently and persistently!

Where ever you are now to where ever your destiny is taking you, the journey is just beginning. I believe that all are destined for greatness, because I don't believe that our God created anyone to end up in the junk pile. I believe that it is our God given responsibility to make choices that lead us to our perfect will in Him.

As you journey with me through these strategies, I pray that you will find a message from God as He has purposed for your heart. If there are things that I have written that you do not agree with please understand that I am writing from my heart and that the message is intended for someone.

Sometimes we take in information today, but the intended use is for a later season. In this case, we store the information until such a time that it is needed. At other times, the information may come of more use for someone that we are close to or a friend that may need our help from time to time. I just believe that "Nothing Just Happens", and you are reading this book for some specific purpose, be it known or unknown at this time. Simply pray and ask God to show you the perfect time for its use.

I believe that success in not just getting from one place to end up at some destination, but success is an ongoing process that never ends. It can take you to new and better heights if you are willing to make some changes. As you have heard in times past, "it is not a DESTINATION, no — no, IT IS A JOURNEY!"

Some people witness success for many years, then get complacent and end up living out their last days with tragedy, simply because they did not accept that mere fact that success is something that you have to wake up to each and every day ready to face. You must start each day with the concept that it is the opportunity of a life time and that you must do today the things that make you happy and the things that will satisfy you tomorrow.

No one knows what the future will bring, but each of us has the opportunity to do something today that we would like to see the results of tomorrow. If you are doing things in the present that you are not proud of or would not want to do if you had it to do over, then stop it! Don't keep fooling yourself. You owe it to you to have the abundant life that was promise to all people everywhere by the only one that is able to keep all His Promises, God!

Being who you really are should be the goal of every person. Releasing your power is understanding what inner ability you have that will lead to being empowered to make the right decisions for your life, that lead to fulfilling your divine purpose. By releasing your power you will find the necessary tools to achieve greatness in the following areas: your personal/spiritual life, your career or occupation, special relationships, your family life and your community life. It is very important that you approach your life with the right Attitude if you expect to have Success. Releasing your power will help you to establish that attitude within you. What is done on the inside, will eventually manifest itself on the outside.

Remember, destiny is calling you from wherever you are right now to your prosperous future. Finding your divine purpose will move you beyond your past. Living according to your purpose is Living the Empowered Life!

Finally, thank you for taking the time to purchase and read this book. We appreciate your kindness and consideration. The ideas, information and suggestions in this book have worked for me and all those that are serious about taking action and making the most of their lives.

Peace and Love to you,
Lilisa J. Williams

Chapter 1

Choosing to Change

"The most effective way to cope with
change is to help create it." **L.W. Lynett**

Have you ever heard yourself saying "if things don't
change around here I'm going to _____?" This statement, no matter what your blank is, is more common than
you and I will ever know. Many people need to make
changes in their lives but not all know how to make the
right changes. In order to reach your divine destiny and
purpose in life, you must be open to change. Not only must
you be willing to change, but you must be willing to keep
on changing until your life is over. Notice I didn't say
"until you get it right!" As soon as you get one thing
straight, then there is always something else to work on.
We are intricate and complex beings and a life time is exactly the right amount of time needed to make us perfect.

Just like companies are constantly pursuing change
and mastering change, you must continuously seek ways to

improve your personal character and qualities. Change at the individual level will eventually impact the wider society.

When I speak of change I am referring to the ability to create or recreate your attitude, actions and feelings. It is my belief that change starts in the heart. It starts in the heart then moves to the mind. From the mind it should move you into action. It should be something that will move you closer to the "true you." Finding the true you could be a long process, or it could be a short process. Only you will know how much time you want to commit to self- development. Some people have to look under years and layers of others telling you who you are. The sad truth is that most people don't know who they really are.

For years, I thought of myself as a loser. I never saw myself as a writer. At the end of this book, I will have two books written and published in less than one year. Not bad for a high school <u>flunk</u> out. *So much for knowing who I wasn't.* The true you is probably not the person you think you are right now. One of the reasons that most people don't know who they are is because they are busy trying to be who they think others believe they are or *should* be. Knowing who you are will empower you to make changes wherever necessary. Every decision and choice you make is taking you closer to who you really are. Be ***extremely*** careful about which choices and decisions you are making.

Releasing your power is about knowing your *true self*. Most people's lives would *explode* if they were only willing to change. You will be empowered to change your life when you realize that you are the only one that can change it. God can show you the direction but you have to make the steps. Without the power to change, our situations, our lives would not only be a mess, but we would be doomed to stay a mess! If I had not changed my behavior from hanging out in night clubs- - - to hanging out in motivational and self-improvement seminars, I shudder to think what my life would be like today.

Over ones lifetime, there are many things we can do that cloud our true attitudes and personalities. The only chance to correct this is to change the ending. You are the director of the movie call "You." You have every right to rewrite the ending! What ever is happening in your life right now, you have the power to change it for the better. You cannot afford to waste another minute complaining and having pity parties. You have to take the charge that God has given you and move onto new territory. He is trying to give you the "promise land." Don't reject it, and please stop complaining! God has placed a power within you that is to help take you to your divine purpose. Once you start walking in your purpose you will *explode!*

In reality, if you want to experience something that you have never experienced before, then, you are going to have do something you have never done before.

In this book, you will find many things that are geared toward empowering and motivating you to make that change. Regardless of your past or current trials, problems or situations, *Choosing to Change* is one of the most important steps you can take to achieving success in your life. You have the power, ability and provision to make the change, my job is to remind you to use what you have and to acquire what you need.

The first thing you must understand is that you were created to be a success! You were born successful. Don't wait to become successful before you start living like a success. Long before I was a paid motivational speaker, I carried myself as a highly paid speaker. Every where I spoke I had the highest level of professionalism, even when I was doing it for free. In actuality, it was never for free because I was paid in "experience." The experience made me an expert and soon people hired me because I was an expert at what I did. I was not "perfect". There is a difference between being perfect and being an expert. For example, expertise is knowing how to do something very well. Perfection is doing something that has no mistakes and no foulups. No one is perfect, but there are many experts.

When it comes to change, don't just make a change for change sake. You have to be driven by your passion and desires to do something that is going to make the world a better place. The world (other people) need what God has put down on the inside of you. If you do not give out of what is in you, your soul, heart and mind will be sick. There has been a force in the world that has convinced you that you are bound to a life of miss-prosperity. Every successful person has had to overcome self denial. As a matter of fact, we are our own worst enemy when it comes to supporting our dreams and goals. Choosing to change may have to start with changing the negative self-talk. Success is no respecter of person. If success could come to others it can certainly come to you.

One of your greatest change assignment is preparing yourself for success. Most people want success, but are not prepared to handle it when it comes. Prior to Tiger Woods winning a golf tournament, he spent many years preparing for it. Before Michael Jordan was successful on the basketball court, he put in many years of preparation. Most people are not successful because they have not prepared themselves for it. If success came to you today, how would you handle it? If others had to prepare for success then you have to prepare also. If it worked for them, it can work for you. Change is often the first and last steps standing between your dynamic future and your present circumstance.

Making changes to various areas of your life will give you power to move to the next level. Don't spend a lot of time waiting for others to tell you that you are empowered. You are empowered when you know that you have a purpose in life and you begin living it. For example, if you want to make a change to some area of your life, weight, education, procrastination, smoking, pride or anything else, it can be accomplished when you exercise your inner strength. Release your power is the use of that inner strength. Just know- - - that your situation will never change until you decide to change. You can try as hard as you like but it will never happen. I know because I tried for over 40 years to find change outside of myself and it didn't work. I finally gave up around age 43 and started looking within. Then I found all the power I needed to make drastic changes to my life.

What I know today is that real change takes place in the mind. By transforming your thoughts, you can overcome all situations. The reason is that new thoughts will lead to new decisions which lead to new behaviors. New behaviors will lead to new outcomes. New outcomes will lead to new satisfaction. New satisfaction will lead to more change. Change moves you to a new place, an elevated place, a place where you no longer fear what's ahead, but begin to look forward to new beginnings. Once the process of change is in place, it will be much easier to flow with it. This constant flow will take you to your divine destiny which is who you are meant to be.

I know- - - -this all sounds too good to be true! You're probably saying 'if its so easy then why isn't everyone doing it?' Good question. I suspect that people have learned over the years how to resist anything that sounds easy. This is a shame because it really is very simple. It starts with deciding that change is something that you *need* to do. To really visualize how powerful change is, pause for just a moment . . . now think of where the world, or even you for that matter, would be if there was *no change*. Unthinkable right?

I'm not telling you anything that it rocket science. This is basic truths that every successful person not only knows, but practices daily.

Without change, you would still be one day old. Without change, we would not have cell phones, (imagine that). Without change, I can't imagine typing this book or making it through the week without "fast food." Change is just a necessary thing. Now stop to think for a moment where our universe would be without change. Certainly, you can sense that change is not only important, but it is necessary. If you really want to know about change just read "Who Moved My Cheese" for a simple but powerful example of what happens when we refuse to change.

Now let us refocus our attention once again on personal change and transformation. Just like the examples above, changes to your mental, physical and spiritual life are equally as important. You cannot afford to force yourself to remain the same when it is natural to change. That is, change for the better! For the most part, you have control over what you think, where you go and the people you keep company with. Thoughts come from what we know. People we keep company with come from who we know and the places we go are based on our choices from a selection of places that we are aware of. Understand that it is your job to pursue changes in your life. It is not someone else's job to make these decisions for you. If you don't like the way your life is going, make a change!

I must counsel you to take some time to consider the results of the change or changes you are seeking to make. Once you get a positive vision of the change, then run with it. Listen to your inner voice and make the right decision and press forward toward your goal. You will amaze yourself with the results. Any goal can be achieve when you have faith and believe in yourself.

Keep in mind that change is a process. Conforming to the process of change involves moving from one place (spiritual, mental, emotional or physical) to another. The process is usually incremental and it may seem like it is not having any effect but just keep plugging
away and soon you will see the end results. Also, change will cause you to exercise your faith. Exercising your faith will help strengthen and empower you. It is not always easy, but time, patience and consistency makes it work.

Making change also involves letting go. You cannot let go of something that you keep holding on to. This is often the problem we face when making a decision to change. We don't want to give up where we are. We have grown accustomed to our old place and fear starts talking to us, trying to convince us that we are better off where we are. Remember what <u>fear</u> really is, <u>False Evidence Appearing Real</u>! It is false, it only appears real. What should you do when your heart is telling you to change, but your mind says "no?" The situation is screaming change, but your mind says "no!" Pray, wait for an answer then make the change despite the fear.

Imagine your success is just on the other side of some decision to change. What do you do? You take a deep breath, close your eyes and take one step forward. Go ahead and try it. Put the book down (just for a minute) close your eyes, take a deep breath and put one foot in front of the other and take another deep breath. That wasn't hard at all. In case you are not able to stand, do a visual. Visualize your self standing and take those same steps. Keep this mental picture every time your heart, situation or opportunity says change and your mind says "no"!

Here is a tip I will throw in for free. Reluctancy is the number one killer of change. If you continue to hesitate and be apprehensive about starting over or getting started at all, it will take you much longer to reach your dreams, goals and your true life purpose. The key is to get control of your mind. Remember, your mind has to do and think what you tell it to. Remember that it won't feel comfortable at first because real change and transformation can only take place by giving something, someone or some place up. Here is another one for free: "once you give it up, you can have it all." Don't be afraid to let go of the past. Better yet, in spite of your fear, let it go any way.

Refusing to *Change* does not only hold you back, but it also can set you back. When it comes to setbacks, I have been through just about every trying situation that a woman can face in her life! Like so many others, my life seemed to have started with many flaws. I truly believe that success in life is not measured by how far you go, but how far you've come. What major changes did it take to get you where you are today or better still, what changes will it take to get you to where you want to go? Or do you even see your self going anywhere? Now is a good time to start dreaming about what you really want to do with your life. After you wake up from your dream, make it happen!!

Many times our childhood is wrought with dysfunction and challenges that cause the dreams we had as children to never be lived out. Though I suffered from child abuse to drug abuse and everything in between, I take the time to dream and live my dreams. I don't let what happened to me to define who I am. I don't allow what I did to define who I am or who I will be. Instead, I define the things that happened to me. I am defined by what I think and I think I like Releasing My Power.

I've had my share of problems and face problems every day, but I overcome them all by spreading the Good News. Sometimes overcoming them means laying them at my Father's Feet. We each have the power to lay down our troubles and pick up success. No, change is not always easy, yet if implemented properly it can have a powerful effect on your life. The secret to change is understanding that change starts with you.

Maybe you're reading this and you feel as though you don't need to make any changes in your life, that you got it all together. Great! I celebrate you and your success. However, maybe there is someone that you know who could benefit from the lessons written in this book. Pass it on to her or him and I thank you for purchasing this copy. Now back to those that are in need (NOW) of lasting change.

Flowing in the Process of Change

If you make a change to some area, any area of your behavior, thoughts or actions, then the situation has to change. It is a natural principle that just works. I don't really know how it works, I just know that it does. Don't take my word for it try it for yourself. Remember, the situation will never change, no matter how much manipulating you do until *YOU* change. Your un-willingness to change is a signal to the situation that it is to remain *unchanged.*

Making a change involves several key steps and key elements. To begin, you must somehow come to the realization that you "must need" to do something different. If you have purchased this book or received it as a gift and are reading it up to this point then it is confirmed that you have achieved the first step to *choosing to change.* After you understand your specific *Need for Changing* this will lead you to the next step where you begin to dismantle the *Difficulty to Changing* and relax as you move to understand the *Power of Changing* in order to *Make Change Last* a lifetime. It is the use of your inner power that will cause you to move through these step and the following elements for a truly purpose-filled and self-actualizing life.

Intertwined in these steps are the following three key elements that impact the overall change process.

The first key element is **acceptance**. You must have faith to accept what you can't change. Faith is a powerful force that will always take you to your next level. You may not be able to see your future, but faith says "not only do I see your glorious future, but you need me if you are going to arrive at it." As you learn to start living according to your faith then you will soon forget how to live in fear. If we allow our fears to keep us from trying something different then we will be prisoners to the situations in life that set us back and keep us back.

The second key element is **courage.** You have to demon-strate courage as you overcome the things in your past. Courage is the part of us that allows us to act in spite of our fears. Fear and faith were not meant to operate at the same time or in the same space. Therefore, you have to make a conscious effort to control your fear. I have lived these forty seven years of my life never knowing that the only thing that drives away fear is knowing who I am in God through Christ Jesus. If you know of another way to live in absent of fear, I would be glad to listen.

The final key element to change is **separation.** You must separate yourself from toxic people, places, things and thoughts. These key elements and the key steps, *Needing to Change, Power to Change* and *Making Change Last* must be operating in your life on a daily basis. In other words, you must make change a *routine.*

Needing to Change

Please keep in mind that: "CHANGE *IS THE ONLY THING THAT IS CONSTANT."* Regardless of how diffi-cult change is – it is something that must be mastered be-cause at some point we all need to make changes. Let's talk a little about these needs.

What is a need? According to the dictionary: a need is something required or desired. Here, we define the word need as: something missing that if present would allow us to reach our ultimate goal and purpose in life.

First, lets remember that needs are very different from wants. Needs will be met one way or the other. Either through your direct actions or through your haphazard un-conscious actions. If the need is not met, the lack will stifle

27

you from growing in some other area. What happens to most people is that they fail to realize that they were created with a specific purpose and goal to reach in life. Fulfilling those needs will lead to finding your true purpose.

What we don't realize is that each of these obstacles or setbacks serves some need that we have within us. As T.D. Jakes says "nothing just happens." For most of us, it is not until we fail at something that we see the need to change and for many of us we have to repeat that situation over and over until we learn our lesson before we can make the *lasting change*, or reach our ultimate goal. That is the need part. The need part is so strong that some will spend years duplicating the same behavior because the need to learn a specific lesson has not yet been learned. The good news is that as soon as that lesson has been learned then the need is met and the person is able to move to the next level.

Keep in mind that as soon as we arrive at the next level we will be met with new and different challenges due to new needs in our lives. As we grow and change we are constantly developing new needs. This is referred to as "Maslow's *Hierarchy of Needs*." This is a basic psychology term for a condition to motivate people to reach their goals in life.

I had the need to be more proactive in my career and personal life. I kept bumping into the procrastination experience until I learned how to be on time and take action in a time efficient manner. Likewise; this need to be on time has helped to make me successful. Our challenges and obstacles, when overcome, will propel us to our purpose. My need to be proactive and on time went unmet until I faced (admitted it) procrastination head on. Now that I have faced it, I must manage it daily to keep in under control. Believe it or not, these challenges and obstacles help to make us strong and shape our lives so that we can make it successfully to our destiny. Such is life. So the sooner we master all the components of life, the better prepared we are to help *design* the type of future that we desire so deeply within our spirits. One that will leave us happy, peaceful, free and whole.

Recognizing that you have a ___need___ to change is a very important first step. It sets the tone for the rest of your private and pubic development. If you truly feel that you do not need to change and are doing exactly what you want and are exactly where you want to be as a person, then you would not be reading this book or perhaps you are reading it because you are my family member and was forced to purchase a copy, none the less, we are never too old or too smart to learn something that we did not know before or did not stop to consider. For a fact, each of us is always seeking to get to a higher place.

When we get to a point that we have learned all that we need to learn and have served every purpose that we have to serve then our time here on earth would be up and we would not be here. For certain, you will not be here any longer than you need to be. So relax, find your purpose, make what ever necessary changes you need to make, and live it. Before we get carried away with change, let's look at some things that might not change.

Accepting What We Can't Change

Face it- - - you can change almost everything about you and almost *nothing* about other people. Please keep this in mind when dealing with others. You can encourage them to change, you can advise them to change and you can even nag them about change. But you cannot make them change! They may ask you to help them change. You have to beware if they do. You cannot help them beyond them sincerely wanting to change. Even if you could get them to change, there is the possibility that they will not stick to it. If a person wants to change it has to come from within, not from without.

Lasting change comes from ones inner drive and desire to change. I have learned that the best thing to do with other people is to listen to them, so that you can know if they are willing to change. If they are, then give them all the help you can. If they are not, then listen to them to show your love and support, but don't let it drain you. Desiring change in others can be very draining, mentally, physically and spiritually.

Some people spend a lot of time trying to change their past. Don't waste time doing that either. The past is over and now is the time to press forward for new things. In order to reach your new success and overcome any setbacks, you must start to *rebuild* your life. Once you make that first step, your divine destiny will kick in and guide and direct you toward your purpose. Acting on your purpose will make you successful. You must start with a fierce drive and motivation. Before motivation and drive can take root, you have to accept and let go of that which has the potential to hold you back. This could be people, things, thoughts or places. In chapter two, we will go into detail on some steps to help you find your purpose in life as we discuss self-assessment.

Overcoming the Past through Change

As a child I can remember being picked on by other kids in the neighborhood and bullied by the class bully.

This abuse lasted almost my entire adolescent and teen years. I guess I got so used to abuse that I accepted it as a common part of my life. I simply learned to adjust to it. I adjusted so well that it wasn't until I was in my early thirties that I was able to make a break from it. I did not know exactly how debilitating this behavior was until I reached my late thirties. By the time I realized what happened, I had already overcome many obstacles that are normally associated with abused children.

That is what I mean by allowing your drive for the future to solve all your past problems. I was so focused on my future that the past did not hinder me. My past was only a problem for other people. Even today, there are still many people that are bothered and troubled by my past. I just pray for those people. If anyone is bothered with your past, it is their problem, not yours. I overcame my past by not living in it. I do talk about it for the sake of motivating others but that is not the same as living in it. Living in the past means that you let it hold you back from being successful today. Eventually I did overcome it and you will overcome your past too.! As soon as you Release Your Power!

Another obstacle that I had to overcome was being a high school drop out. For years, I lived feeling like a failure educationally. I constantly failed class after class, year after year. I eventually gave up. At the age of 16, I became a high school drop out. Dropping out of school for me was devastating, not to mention embarrassing, and it left me feeling extremely disconnected from the rest of my peers. I remember my closest friend in high school, Teresa, not only graduated, but went to college. To top it off, she was very smart. I remember times when we would get together she would be talking about her calculus classes. At the time, I did not even know what calculus was. I had an idea that it

31

was some kind of math. I was too embarrassed to ask her what it was.

After drifting for about two years in what seemed like a daze, I followed the path of my younger sister, and enrolled myself in a GED course and after several months was prepared to take and pass my GED, the high school equivalency exam. For the first time in my life, I felt a true sense of accomplishment. The sad part is that it did not last too long. Before long, I was back on the treadmill of setbacks, pitfalls and failures. I still had a lot of changing to do. For some reason, I just did not get it.

At age 32, I went back to school. I started taking classes toward my associate's degree at Essex County College in Newark, NJ. There, I was enrolled in the lowest level remedial math class offered. I aced that class and every class all the way through to 2 sessions of Calculus. I could not believe that the girl who once did not know what Calculus was, was now getting straight A's in the subject. Through perseverance and a new attitude, I was able to overcome all my academic setbacks.

In reality, I had released my power (inner ability) on the way I thought of learning, education and teachers. When I was growing up I hated school! I thought teachers were "a joke" and that school was a waste of my time. My attitude is totally different today. Today, I not only value teachers, but also education and the institutions by which education is administered. Believe it or not, I am a college professor. How's that for knowing who you really are. . . .

Cutting "Unhealthy" Soul-Ties

A "soul-tie" (as used here) is a word used to describe a close relationship between a man and a woman. It is when two souls are intertwined through extremely strong emotions.

Therefore, a soul-tie can be created when two people enter an intimate (sexual) relationship. The problem with creating soul-ties, is when it is done between two "unmarried" people. After the relationship has ended the soul-tie that was created can last for years. This soul-tie can become psychological and emotional baggage that could possibly hinder the stability and success of future relationships. The work that it takes to cut soul-ties can be daunting. There is Power that is from God that can lead to the successful severing of all such ties and their potential damage. These unhealthy ties must be cut!

I thought the hardest thing from my past to overcome was men. From my early teenager years I got involved with boys in hopes of having someone to make me "feel special." Trying to have a relationship with a boy was just plain foolish. I had no education, no plans for my future and no real self worth. I pretty much fell for anyone that told me what I wanted to hear - - - and they knew it. I consider all of my relationships, prior to my marriage, to be one setback after another. For instance, I was once involved with a man that tried to kill me simply because of his personal jealousies and insecurities towards "*his woman.*" I began to submit to the fact that I was never going to find a man that truly loved me just for me. Every man that I met, prior to my husband, had some string attached. Usually that string was sex and violence.

I finally figured out that they were looking for someone to take all their pain out on. Hurting people hurt others. I did not learn this until 1990 when I took my first Psychology course in college. I was blown away when I figured how much time I had wasted allowing others to take their problems out on me. I was about to give up and call it quits when the words of my mother rang in my ears: "if you make your bed hard you have to lie in it." I never forgot her words. I used them to push me beyond my past and to drive me straight to my success. I figured it was time for me to make a change and start to- - - "make my bed soft." I figured as long as I had to lie in it I may as well make it as comfortable as possible.

That's when I realized that I had power to improve my condition. Suddenly, I began telling myself that "you can be more but you will have to change." I liked the sound of being more. I didn't know much about how to make change, so I started praying for a change. Wouldn't you know it, change just showed up. Glory to God. He is always on time! He is never late!

I share this information with you so that you get a clear picture of why I felt the need to write this section of the book about overcoming the past by changing. So when I write about the do's and don'ts for overcoming your guilt and shame of your past, I have the personal experiences to back up what I teach. Having dropped out of school, having been abused as a child and getting involved in several relationships that turned out to be 'BAD news' I can honestly say I have been to hell and back. These situations left me with the feeling that I was not very good at anything and that it would be impossible for me to have any kind of real success in my life. Then I learned how to overcome my past. It is for this reason that Philippians 4:8 always reminds me of who I am in Christ and Philippians 3:13-14 reminds me to let go of my past and to press forward.

What it boils down to is that I was sick and tired of doing the same ole thing. I wanted something new and I finally realized that I had to make a change to get it. I had wasted far too much time trying to attain success with my methods and schemes, however, nothing I did worked or had a lasting affect. Not only that, but everything I tried seemed to end up a worst predicament.

I finally realized that the change that I sought could only be found in the word of God. I was convince of this because I had looked everywhere else. I had tried to find it in men, sex, drugs and money. It just was not there. I'm not glorifying what I have been through, its just that I recognize how the world had tried everything possible to keep me from my destiny. This book is a verbal heartfelt thanks to God for not allowing the enemy to triumph over me. Through this book and the work that it took to complete it, I have overcome my greatest setback and have tasted great success. Growing up the "class dummy", I never thought I would have achieved writing a book or doing motivational seminars. Just goes to prove anyone can change anything!

My past is still what it is. I was a high school drop out. I was molested and involved in sexual abuse as a child. However, today I do not live in the past. I have overcome the past not by changing it, but by changing my future. Today I have advanced degrees and am married to a good, kind, saved and loving man. We are able to overcome because we were made to be more than conquerors!

The Difficulty of Change

Let's face something right up front. Change has its challenges. The million dollar question on everyone's mind is "why is change so difficult?" Change is tough, but not impossible. We will explore this question, but I caution you to keep in mind the fact that it would take more than a book of this magnitude to fully address all the possible reasons and explanations as to why change is considered tough.

What we will attempt to do here is to spark a drive and fire within you that will set you on an endless journey to finding all the answers you need to fulfill *your* purpose and to reach success as you define it for *your* life. You have the rest of your life to pursue all the aspects of change.

To begin we will look at this difficulty from the point of view that change happens so quickly. The simple fact is that the world, people and things are changing all the time. They never stop. Trying to adjust could become difficult and frustrating. Since we are "spiritual beings trying to have a human experience", we run into difficulty when we are out of balance with our purpose and His perfect will for our lives. We have to learn how to balance adapting to new things while managing our contentment in where we are until we get to where we are going. As our world becomes more complex and technology continues to spin our society and world faster and faster, it is imperative that we learn all the tools we can to help us in this battle to keep up with change.

Other factors that make change difficult are our needs to be accepted by others. When we do not sense that others will support us in some new idea that we may have for ourselves, we start to feel pressured and become reluctant to make the change that we had envisioned. This is the greatest tragedy of all, failing for fear of what others will think of us.

Also, if the thing that we want to change is a part of our personality or character that is benefiting others, they will put up road blocks to keep the change from happening. Most of this sort of work is done unconsciously, so there is generally no way to prevent it. And by the time we realize what is happening so much time has passed, and we lose sight of what our initial goal or dream was.

Fear is probably the number one factor that makes change difficult. The unknown is sometimes just too scary. We allow fear to keep us from changing. Sometimes we are fearful of letting go of what we have become accustom to doing. We simply become attached to the familiar. We set up our own mental road blocks without recognizing what we are doing.

Whatever the reasons for the resistance to change, it is something that we must deal with and eventually get to the point that we can make change smoothly and make it work for us. The best way to do this is to start small.

Start making small changes in your life to get comfortable with making changes. As you grow in your personal development, you will learn to handle bigger projects. Keep in mind that you are not the first person nor will you be the last to have to make significant changes in your life. All successful people make change as if it were there own design. They have come to live with the fact that in order to have what they want they must change some things and do it quickly.

Change is not just difficult for individuals it is also difficult for businesses and groups. Consider the difficulty that sales people have in trying to get customers to switch from using one product to something new. I still use products simply because my mother used them, not necessarily because they are the best products. Companies realize this, that is why they will sometimes upgrade the brand rather than develop a new product.

And how about the change that most every body wants to avoid- - - - getting older? What about relationships and marriages, where one spouse or partner refuses to change their behavior, regardless of its destructive nature? Two things that I have learned about change: 1) we love to change when we can readily see the benefit up front for us, 2) if there is not immediate benefit, then we work very hard at resisting change.

As an example of change and the resistance thereof, lets consider the following statements. "Its so hard to change, I tried numerous times to: quit smoking; lose weight; change my eating habits; get my husband or wife to attend church; get my children to do better in school and/or at selecting positive peers and role models." In all or any of the above statements the person is speaking the direction of their lives. It is something psychologist call the "self-fulfilling prophecy." This is where whatever you say will come true. If you say you can't quit smoking then you are already defeated. Whenever we speak, we are speaking what will happen. The choice is yours, so "choose life!" We can write our own ticket with the power that comes from God - - -- - through our words! After all—they have life!

Yet when our mind is made up about anything, that thing can be accomplished through change and commitment. I believe we were designed that way on purpose so that when we are standing in the Judgment no one can use the excuse that someone else should take blame for what we ourselves have done. Likewise, if we are the ones with the control over what we choose, then we must take full responsibility for how we choose and which decisions we make. Hard as it might be to change, it is no where near impossible.

Change can also seem difficult when we consider that

the process of change can create a large amount of work and mass huge amounts of personal effort and time. Working on ourselves will leave us little to no time to try and change others.

The bottom line is that change is inevitable and we must learn as best we can how to manage it in our lives so that we can take full advantage of its many benefits. For the purposes of this book, we will focus on the positive affects of Change. Our hope is that as time passes you will start to see some true value in embracing change. Now join me as we look briefly at some points about the power of change and how to make change last.

Power of Change

The power of change comes when you understand who and only who gives you the power to change. The power that I am talking about here can only be experienced by accepting the work of the Holy Spirit. If you are reading this book and don't understand who the Holy Spirit is then visit my website at www.brandnewbeginnings.org for more detail. I have come too far to leave out the main reason that I am here and doing this and all other work that I do. Maybe you just want to change your hair color or your eye color, in that case you don't need the work of the Holy Spirit. But I had to change from a sexually promiscuous child into a virtuous woman. From a high school dropout to an MBA graduate. These changes and others could only be achieved with the help of a holy God. People want to attribute their success to other factors like their level of education, growing up in the proper environment and financial status. But without God, where would their finances, education or family get them. All these things will fade away then what will they be left with?

Something magical happens when you line up with God's plan for you to receive power to turn your life into something prosperous. He sent His son to die so that you and I would have the right to an abundant life. I don't know about you but I want everything that God promised and everything that Jesus Christ suffered, died and rose for.

Power to feel confident enough to make changes only comes when you are in the center of God's perfect will for your life. Think about it, how do you see your self right now relative to your success and your being lined up with God? Be honest with yourself. What is your life saying? Prior to knowing the power of God, my life wasn't saying anything! The moment you make up your mind to make a change, even the slightest change, you are in position for your whole life to change for good!

I remember thinking that my life would never change. I thought that people would always respond to me as they had in the past and that I would always make decisions that led me down a path to failure, hurt and loneliness. In reality, my life successes started with my first step toward making a change. Think about a snowball rolling down a hill. When it starts it is very small and as it rolls it grows bigger and bigger. Each time that it takes a roll it picks up more snow making it grow. Think of each roll as another change. That is what happens to our lives. Compare your life to the snow ball. As you make changes your life will grow bigger and bigger. Also as the snowball is rolling down hill it picks up speed and momentum.

That is what our life looks like as we make changes;

we pick up speed and momentum. People start to come into our life and add something to us and we continue to grow. Even the negative people teach us something. If nothing else we learn what not to do or be. Try to stay away from negative people. They drain your energy. It takes energy to live your dreams and reach your goals. If you allow other people to drain all your energy how will you accomplish what you need to get it all done?

My success began the minute I decided to make a change. My oldest sister, Jan, once told me something that I never ever forgot, she said "There is nothing more powerful than a made up mind." The hardest step to make in any change effort is the first step. You are guaranteed to fail if you fail to get started. Even if you want to make a change deep in your heart, but are unable to make the first step it will never happen. "I can assure you that it probably won't drop out of the sky." If it does, please let me know! This is where the power in change lies. When you take that first step there is so much power in it, you will be motivated to keep on stepping. You have to learn how to make the first step. After you make the first step, keep stepping!

The first step has to take place in your heart. After you have prayed about it and you are at peace with your decision, run with it. Before you make a change in your action or behavior you must change your thinking. For me, I had to make a change in the way I was living my life and change the things in which I was participating in. As I look back over my life, I can truly say that this was the toughest of all my challenges. Choosing to change. If you are like most of us, you may not recognize the total power of choosing to make a change.

Sometimes, even the slightest change can have a powerful impact on your life. Especially when you are not so certain about the outcome of your choice. You only have that gut feeling that change is the right thing to do. That small inner voice that you rarely listen to, yet so clear, is the right choice. Go on and follow that inner voice, what do you have to lose? Consider a huge ship bellowing down the ocean, a slight movement of the helm will cause the direction of the ship to change.

Change is the kind of thing that everyone can talk about but few people are successful at getting it right. This is evident by the amount of self-help books, workshops and training seminars on the subject of change. The real truth is that most people spend much more time resisting change that they ever spend on making change. I have learned to be a lover of change. I have learned to allow myself to be inspired by change. "If you want your life to be something it has never been before, you will have to do something you have never done before!!"

Making Change Work

Making change work is all about making it a regular practice in our lives until it becomes second nature to perform the changed behavior. With the right frame of mind making changes to your life can be fun and exciting. One way to do this is to embrace it fully. That means fully forgetting the mistakes, failures and pains of your past.

When I made the change from allowing my body to be used by the persons who promised me the most love, it was easy as I practiced letting go of the past. After I got into the habit of turning down the company of others, I got excited about my power to "just say no." That power motivated me to take more control of my own life. Its funny how when a seed is planted, it will grow and a seed had been planted in me by my heavenly Father and as it got watered the seed grew into a strong mighty tree. Like with a natural tree, it grows above ground, and its roots are growing beneath the ground where the real nutrients come from that sustain its life and makes it strong. Likewise, we have a root system that is planted in the Almighty God and He will supply all our needs and His love and power will sustain us in every situation.

Begin to accept and apply the changes to your heart, mind and body. Begin to see change for what it is. Begin to see the spiritual aspect of change not just the physical. Take into account that without change the world would cease to exist. If the world were to stay stagnate, then there would be no tomorrow. Keep in mind though, that change can take any amount of time. So don't use your finite mind to fix change into a limited space of time.

Count your blessings when some things seem to change over night with little or no effort on your part. That's the momentum that is driving that snowball as it rolls down hill. Don't forget to acknowledge the other times in your life when change may take a considerable amount of time, time to make meaningful changes can have powerful effects. Everything you've learned was a result of making small changes.

Consider how you had to change from drinking most of your food from a bottle to eating your food with a spoon or fork. Then you had to change your diet from mostly milk and cereal to things like hot dogs and pork & beans and potatoes. As you continued to grow you had to changed in many ways and at different times and stages in your life. Change will work if you work it.

You changed from having your caretakers do everything for you to doing things for yourself and from being by yourself to having a mate. These are just some examples of the changes that you have already mastered. Now if you could master something as complicated as standing and walking from a time when all you could do was lay, cry and poop then you should be able to handle what ever else life may bring. I give these examples as a demonstration of how common change is for human beings.

Other areas of change include jobs, careers, living arrangements and as women we change hairdos more than any thing else. Its not so much the change as it is our attitude toward the change that will determine its success and ultimately our success. Stop to think for a minute, what have you *not changed lately*? The key to lasting change is to stay committed to the change. Just like when we are trying to change our eating habits or our exercising habits- - - the thing that puts us back in the same position is our own lack of commitment to the changed behavior. Without will power and discipline it will be very hard to make any lasting change. The only real solution is to work at the changed behavior until it becomes second nature and never forget where your strength and power comes from.

Now that we have some insight to this matter of change and want to start making changes in our lives that will take us to our successful destiny lets consider some of things that we might need or want to change.

What do you want to change?

_____

_____

Changing People, Places, Things, and Thoughts (PPTT)

When we change the people we hang around with, the places we go, the things we do and the thoughts we think on, our lives *will* be *changed!* You can pick up any motivational self-help book you desire (starting with the Bible) and you will find that this is a popular truth. By following this precept, simple as it may seem, you can begin to put things in order. Start by changing the people that you have been associating with if they are not moving to the next level. Once you have cleared the negative people out of your life, then look to stop hanging around the same places that have not moved you to the next level or have not brought you any real satisfaction. One thing is that you have to be very honest with yourself. We all have some things that we do that we know are not benefiting us and therefore we should let these things go! It may be difficult at first because we have grown accustomed to them, but they are not serving us any present or future value and they don't add to our purpose so why hold on to them?

Our thoughts are another critical area that we must learn how to control. We must let go of any and all negative thoughts. Therefore, we should spend time alone reflecting on all the thoughts that come into our minds on a daily basis. When you find yourself thinking about or coming up with a negative thought or a thought that is not centered on advancing you to your next level then arrest that thought and delete it right away.

Don't give your thoughts the chance to impact your behavior or your speech. Picture the way in which we use our email systems for example. When I receive an email

45

and do not recognize the sender or the subject is not appealing to me, I immediately delete it. It may be carrying a virus and I don't want my files or computer system ruined. We should be just as diligent with our thoughts, so that they have no time to grow and ruin our minds. The word of God cautions us to "think only on things that are pure, lovely and peaceful."

Yes, real change will start with the power within us being released on ourselves and then it will spill over on others. Releasing Your Power will eventually become the thing that you do on a regular basis. As you begin to develop into the thing or things that God has created you to do the power of your life will be felt for many years to come!

You were created for a great reason and the talents, skills and abilities that will bring your greatness to fruition lies in your ability to *Release Your Power!* Don't wait another minute, get up and get to it! NOW! Let today be the first day to becoming who you really are. I will be here praying for your success!

I may not know who you are - - - - but I know that YOU ARE SOMEBODY GREAT!

Now Record Some of the Successful Changes You Have Made over Your Life Time.

_____

_____

_____

_____

_____

_____

_____

_____

_____

_____

_____

_____

_____

_____

_____

_____

_____

_____

_____

_____

_____

_____

_____

_____

Chapter 2

Spending Time With Yourself

"Know thyself" means this, that you get acquainted
with what you know, and what you can do."
Menander

DON'T HIDE, LOOK INSIDE. You can only hide
from what's on the inside of you for so long. Sooner or
later you will have to face you. You've faced everybody
else, now it is time to spend some time facing you. We
have dealt with one of the hardest steps first, that being
making a change. If we can get that step mastered then
there will be smooth sailing from here on out. Therefore,
you should take your time in working through this book, so
that you allow the concepts, rather they be new to you or
new to you applying them, to take root down in your inner
man or woman. As equally as important as making changes
and cleaning house, so to speak, is this matter of needing to
know exactly who you are, what you are about, and my fa-
vorite, whose you are.

In order for me to have made the types of changes
that were made in my life, from drug addiction to sobriety,
from physical and emotional abuse to standing up for myself and saying no, from lack of knowledge to an abundance
of educational accomplishments, from a pitiful spirit to

49

godly knowledge and wisdom and from the gutter-most to the uttermost, I had to do some serious introspection. I admit, this did not happen over night, nor was it a task that was completed in five or ten years, as a matter of fact it is ongoing and continues every day. There is something new, regardless of how insignificant it may seem to me at the time, that I learn about myself each and everyday.

Granted, some or most of the things, are not always things that I am most proud of, yet they are areas that need my attention, so I am thankful that they have surfaced. I believe we are all here on assignment to fix ourselves. God gave us a mirror, so that we can look in it and fix what we see of ourselves. When I stopped trying to fix my husband, nieces and nephews and others, I had time to work on Lilisa.

God provides us with many mirrors and numerous opportunities to look at who we really are and to correct the things that are not pleasing to Him. He has strategically placed people in our lives to help with this process. The problem is that sometimes people take their roles in correcting you too seriously. When they do this it often turns us off to the idea of fixing what they have pointed out. But if we are honest with ourselves, we might notice a pattern in the faults that they point out to us. My mother used to say "a hundred Frenchmen can't be wrong." I know she was quoting this but I am not aware of where she heard it. That's just how she was, always training us through a quote. I remember when she used to tell me that "nothing hurts a duck but its bill." Instead of just saying, "shut up, you talk too much" she would recite that quote. It took me a while but I finally got it. She used quotes like this to make us think. I am very thankful that she did.

50

We can learn a lot about ourselves from taking into account what others tell us. However, it is also wise to have your own personal perspective of your faults and weaknesses. When you compare what others say with what you see then you will have a pretty accurate assessment of who you really are. Keep in mind that no matter how accurate yours and others assessments are, they are incomplete and subordinate to what God has to say about who you really are. Until He reveals who you are then you only have a shadow of you. As you meditate and reflect on you, look at the negative, positive and unique qualities that make you. Remember, don't get to hung up on who you are because you are always changing.

Spending time alone will help you deal with the hard stuff. Let's say for the sake of argument that you do not take the time to assess who you really are, the self that you are when no body is looking. Life has a way of putting you in situations that you will be forced to look at yourself. Sometimes we have to land on our backs to take that inner look. Try to avoid that forcing if possible, just take a few moments a day and reflect on what you did, said and whose life you have touched with kindness and joy. I hope you did not hurt anyone today and if you did go and apologize to the person. Apologizing to people that we have hurt or offended frees us from the burden of guilt and shame. Spending time in seclusion will give you the opportunity to see what you are doing.

It may sound simple just to sit and reflect on who and what we are, but try it and get back to me on just how easy it is. If you are like most of us it is not so easy. This is mostly due to the fact that there is so much "stuff" in our lives that has built up over the years. It can become hard to look at it and accept. Changing it may seem impossible. It is. That is why you need outside help from God. Only He can help us with the truly hard and impossible things. Tell yourself, "I can do all things through Christ that strengthens me." I remember thinking, "Lord, I cannot write a book." He said, "no you can't but I can write it through you." Today I have two books written, self published and selling. For a high school flunk out — not bad!

Most of us do not want to deal with the things we have packed in our respective bags. For years, I tried to avoid the fact that I was the victim of sexual abuse, molestation and rape. Like a lot of people, it was difficult to unpack these things because I feared that it would destroy me if I looked at it. Plus, I did not know how to deal with what had happened in my life. The best thing was to try and forget about it. However, trying to forget lead me to drugs, prostitution, low self esteem and a host of other negative behaviors. I finally learned to understand what happened- - - not just dismiss it. This eventually helped me to become who I really am.

Its like that junky closet or that unresolved bitterness that we hold against someone who has hurt or betrayed us. You simply try to forget these things ever happened. Then one day you can no longer avoid it and you realize that you have to face it and resolve it. Then real victory comes when you overcome it and begin to use it to empower others. Telling others your painful situations help you to see that you are not alone and that others experience the same stuff that you thought was leading to your demise.

So, what do you do with the unwanted things that you find out about yourself as you are doing all this self-assessment? The key is to deal with each piece you find in the bag separately. As each piece of un-forgiveness, jealously, pride, rejection, self-pity, abuse and whatever else you have been holding on to from the past is revealed to you- - - follow these steps for letting it go:

Step one: Acknowledge what happened without blaming anyone (blaming will not make the thing that has happened not have happened). Acknowledge that "It Ain't About You!" It had to happen- - - - why not you? Now you have a testimony, something to help others with.

Step two: Accept the part you played or accept the part that others played (without blame and bitterness) holding on to bitterness takes up space in your heart that could be used for positive actions.

Step three: Look at where you are now and where you would like to be, then work on getting there. Begin seeing yourself as God sees you.

Step four: Don't Look Back! This is the critical step. Sometimes when you look back you go back. Don't go back until you are totally healed of your past. Only go back after you have healed, and only to save others. Don't go back to show off.

Take these steps as often as needed until you can do them without even thinking. Do them until they become habit. Once you know the process, you can use it on any situation that tries to hold you down or hold you back. Don't be afraid to have faith in your prosperous future.

If you need counseling to go through these steps by all means do some research and get referrals from trusted friends and family members.

The Value of Self-Awareness

Spending time alone so that you can get to know what you are really all about should not come simply as a result of loneliness, incarceration or hospitalization. This act of spending time alone should be initiated by you as a welcomed activity and used as a time to meditate and reflect on your inner most qualities. It is a way to get a clear and in-depth look into your soul and a method for getting in touch with your spirit. For there, you will find all the treasures to your life. "Where your heart is there is your treasures also." There you will find the keys that will unlock the treasures to your future and your success.

If for some reason you find yourself alone due to one of these above circumstances, then count it a joy that you will now at least get the time to do something that you should have been doing all along. If you happen to be laid up then use your time wisely, preparing for the day when you will be up and about.

However, I am specifically dealing with making a choice to take some time aside from your busy schedule and take a look within. In order to benefit from self assessment you can start by doing the following:

1. turning off the T.V.
2. turning off the radio
3. unplugging the phone
4. don't answer the door

There is simply no other way to take time alone with your

self but to do it! If you wait for your schedule to get less hectic, it never will, at least mine didn't. Don't worry, you will later reap all the rewards that come from spending time getting to know who you are. Remember, we are on this journey to fix ourselves. How can you fix what you don't know is broken?

Living to release your power requires you to live a life where you value self-assessment and doing something about what you assess. After all, what would be the value of doing an assessment only to discover that what you have uncovered you are not willing to do anything about. What a waste of time that would be! Yet, this happens all the time. Sometimes we find problems in some area of our life but we don't want to expend the effort that it would take to correct it. In this case, it is often easier to just ignore it or to blame others. Blaming others takes the focus off what we need to do. It is called "making excuses". Someone once told me that "Excuses are the nails that are used to build a house of failure".

Changing, assessing and all the other things that it will take to move you from living in fear and start living abundantly through your faith will not happen over night. Do understand that this is a process. One that may take weeks, months or even years to master. But what else will you be doing for the next several years. So why not get started on something that is sure to have positive future affects. Not just for you but for your entire family and many others that have been placed on this earth for you to touch.

You are the single most important person in your life. You cannot do one single thing for another until you have been successful with your own problems and circumstances.

And you cannot work on what you don't know is a problem.

Please do not think for one minute that I did this work on my own. I did nothing outside of what God allowed me to do through Him, using His power and strength I was able to live out my dreams. Writing this book, starting a business and starring in a movie are just examples of this fact.

If we are not all that we can be to ourselves then how can we ever expect to be anything of value to others. For example, most people are not able to give their children and mates any real and true love because they have neglected to first study themselves and find out what it takes to love. This is a tragedy for most people today. However, all is not lost in your case. Now that you have decided to work on your life and to create a future that will be both rewarding and fulfilling you can enjoy yourself, enjoy others and have them enjoy you.

Power of Self Assessment

Now that you have spent an hour or two a week alone just reflecting on your past, present and dreaming of your future now you are ready to move to your purposeful future.

Try a little game with yourself where you remember all the good and bad things that have happened to you since as early as you can remember. Keep in mind that this is just an exercise and not meant to harm or hurt anyone. Remember that anything that has happened in the past has already happened and cannot hurt you now, these are only memories. So you may feel free to relax and let your mind wonder. Before you start you may want to meditate on the fact that God loves you no matter what you have been through and He has already prepared the way for you to be forgiven of any wrong that you have done or has been done toward you. You have His assurance on this through the Death of His only Begotten Son. His death and resurrection is our spiritual, physical and written guarantee that He has not only forgiven us for what we have done, but also for what we will do. No one, including the highest government or political official or high priest, can give this guarantee.

The power lies in not just knowing who you are, but the power lies in being who you *REALLY* are. The power of assessment will come when you take what you learn and turn it into real life situations. Waiting for someone to make you who you are will not give you power. Others do not know all there is about you. You have to spend time alone and get in a quite spot so that God can show you who you are for real. He will reveal, often in pieces, your true purpose in life. *Jeremiah 29:11*

I believe God uses pieces because we would not be able to handle the whole thing at once and it builds our faith in Him and we have to depend on Him for each step in the process. God knows that if He gave us the entire plan that we would run ahead of Him and probably end up messing things up. We must keep in mind that ultimately it is His plan. "We were created for His good pleasure".

You will need the power of God to look at many of the things that have happened to you in your past. I was molested and sexually abused until I was 17 years old by a family member. This was a person that I loved very much and looked up to. I did not understand how what he was doing was wrong. I just did not understand it. It was just a natural part of what my childhood included. When I turned 18 years old, for some reason it stopped. I never questioned what happened to me. I just tried to forget it. That lasted for many years. Then when I was thirty three years old, I was taking a psychology class and the topic of sexual abuse came up. Other students were sharing their stories and the pain that they now live with that was caused by what had happened to them. I noticed at that time that I was not affected by what happened to me the way they were describing their pain. I came to realized that God had set me free from any bad side affects that usually happen to former abused children.

I share this story as an example of how you can exercise your inner power to overcome the things that have happened in your past no matter how bad it was. I am so thankful that God loves me enough that He gave me another chance to have the life that He had initially prepared for me.

Leave No Stone Unturned

As you begin your assessment process realize that it must me done with patience. You will have just enough time on earth to fix everything if you start now and don't give up. Don't do like some and think that because you have been working on yourself for the first 20 or 30 years that you have it all together. Truly successful minded people know that "success is not a destination but a journey". The work that needs to be done on each of us has as its final result perfection. We will not be perfect until He comes back. Therefore, you have time to look at every area of your life. Start by keeping in mind that what we notice about others is usually a fault in us. This will give you a good starting point for which to begin your change process.

Start by making a list of who you think you are, who you are when nobody's looking and who others have said you are. This list should also include things that you have done. Be spontaneous in listing things about you. After you make a list of all these things, organized them into the following categories:

1) Things that I want to forget.
2) Things that I want to remember.
3) Things that I must forgive and forget.
   (keep in mind that He has forgiven us freely so we too should forgive those who have hurt us freely)
4) Things that I want to improve.

Use this list to point out areas of weakness and areas of strength. This list should show you your positive attributes and which ones you need to let go of.

Learn to become your own cheerleader. I celebrate all my victories, both small and large. Then I always give praises to my heavenly Father, who alone is worthy of all my praise. He and he alone delivered, freed, and kept me from destruction for such a time as this. Had He not been there, I would not be here today writing this book. He is Awesome!!

Above all, it is time to learn to love yourself. You can't spread what you don't have. You have to spread love not just wait for others to show that they love you. If you spread it, it will come back to you. We reap what we sow!

If you are one of those people who aren't used to spending time with yourself it can be very scary and lonely at first. But like everything else, it takes getting used to. Remember, once you start the process make every effort to keep it up. One fun way to start the process is to take long bubble baths. We spend time helping everyone and loving everyone else, and often, especially women, we ourselves are neglected. Also, this can be a time to relax and reflect on your day, week, month and eventually year. Always try to remember that the time spent alone is not punishment. It is a time to get to know your inner most self and a time to show yourself some real love.

All of the answers to our happiness and success is inside of us. If we do not take the time to get to know us then we will spend time trying to find happiness outside of ourselves which is **impossible.** No matter how long you may look and who you may turn to you will never find the answers to your problems or the solutions to your life by looking to others. No one can give you the keys to your heart other than God, the one who created you. Those keys were placed in each of us as a gift to lead us to our divine purpose in life. So don't look out, look in, to find your happiness and your purpose. By taking the time to look inside you will gain all the tools to fix what shows up on the outside!

Record Areas of Your Inner Self that YOU would like to change and Accomplishments that you would like to celebrate.

_____

_____

_____

_____

_____

_____

_____

_____

_____

_____

_____

_____

_____

_____

_____

_____

_____

_____

_____

_____

_____

_____

_____

*Record Areas of Your Inner Self
that YOU would like to change and Accomplishments that you would like to celebrate.*

_____

_____

_____

_____

_____

_____

_____

_____

_____

_____

_____

_____

_____

_____

_____

_____

_____

_____

_____

_____

_____

_____

_____

_____

_____

_____

Chapter 3

Writing It Down

"Write the Vision and Make it Plain." **Habakkuk**

There is something magical about putting things in black and white. It seems that writing something down on paper makes it more permanent. As if writing it down will make the very thing happen. I can honestly say that there are things that I've written down in a journal some 10 to 12 years ago, without any real evidence that the thing would come to past, yet I have lived to see these things manifest themselves in my life. Before I ever had any kind of career in higher education and with no formal education myself, I wrote, as a class assignment, in a journal that I wanted to work in a college. Today I have a job at a local community college and have been teaching college classes since 1998. Wow! Talk about the power of writing down our dreams and desires. It's as if there is some "self-fulfilling prophesy" regarding writing. If you write it down, it is bound to happen.

I think that one reason this happens is that it takes

great strength and effort (for most of us) to make note of our thoughts. The very process of writing frees you to see clearly what is happening around you. Writing creates thinking and deciding to change your thinking can renew your entire life! What a concept. A new life. Writing will also touch on your heart and your mind, so the thing that you write is constantly with you. With all three working in unison, mind, spirit and body, is bound to bring you to a greater understanding of your life's work. You may not understand this all at once, but revelation will come over time.

There is certainly more then one reason for writing down what is on our minds and in our hearts including the benefit of leaving a recorded message for others to learn and grow from. Where would we be if people did not take the time to write about various things throughout history? We would always have to start from scratch when we want to do anything. How awful that would be and very time consuming. No— writing things down is definitely a good and worthy practice. I can't imagine my life if the Ancient people had not been inspired to record the events in the Bible.

The Benefit of Journaling

Keeping a journal is a way to remind ourselves that our goals and dreams do change over time and a way to remember the many things that come in our minds on a daily basis. Also, writing helps us to get used to making plans by putting it in writing. It is something about the art of writing that convicts our hearts and can ultimately bring us closer to our goals.

In early historical times, writing was highly praise, mostly because it was the only way to communicate long distance. Unlike today where we have phones, TV, games, music and many other forms of communication. In those days if you could write you were highly paid because you had the ability to serve as a medium for communication. Not everyone had that opportunity in those days. Today, just about everyone has the basic tools for communication, at least everyone in this country and any other highly industrialized nation. Yes, writing has a very rich and long history and will not be able to fully get its true value in this short book but by all means if your curiosity has been peaked then you owe it to yourself to continue your search in this field. I have found it to be a very fascinating and extremely enlightening activity.

If someone had told me 5, 10 or 20 years ago that I would write I book, I would have looked at them like they were crazy. But today, all I think about is writing, mostly because I have this deep desire to share everything that God has allowed me to learn and know. Over the past 5 years, I have used writing for the sole purpose of turning my life around. My recommendation is that you do the same. Let writing be a source that will help you by moving you to the next level. Keep in your journal all your future aspirations then review what you have written from time to time. You will be AMAZED!

Another benefit to journal writing is that it gives you an opportunity to write down things that you want to stop doing or things you want to be free from doing. For instance when I wanted to stop being unforgiving this was something that I wrote about. Or when I wanted to stop being a procrastinator, I listed this in my journal along with thoughts that I wanted to stop thinking and places that I wanted to stop going. Writing it down was my way of laying it down.

Obedience is Better than Sacrifice

The first time I was instructed to keep a journal was 1990 for an English 101 class in junior college. I was frightened to death of having to write. I was not accustomed to writing and had no clue that I would someday enjoy writing to the point that I would write a book. I was only doing it because I had to get a grade for completing the assignment of keeping a journal. As it turned out, every class that I had in the next two years required me to keep some sort of journal.

All the professors would say the same thing, "It will improve your writing skills". I've come to learn that they were all right! Now I write because I have something that I want to communicate to others. Without the early days of journal writing, I don't know where I would be in the writing arena today. I am just thankful that I was serious enough about my grades that I bought the journal and forced myself to write. In the beginning, it started with just a sentence or two and continued to grow. Before long, I could sit and write several pages at one time. I have continued the habit of journal writing over the past 12 years.

Whenever you have to do something that you are not used to doing it will feel awkward. There are stages that we all go through when we try something for the first time. At first we are reluctant and we have to make ourselves do it. Then we feel awkward until we have completed the task several times. After we get used to the new idea and have done it over and over, we get comfortable and even may come to like the new activity. Then the reverse happens should we build up the habit and have to end it. Like the old saying, "habits are easier to form than they are to break." It only takes 21 days to create a habit, that is if you do it 21 days in a row. Try that the next time you want to create a habit of something.

Believe and You Shall Receive

One thing for sure, journal writing will be a chore if you think that it is. If you allow yourself to relax and accept it as something that you will enjoy doing then the task will be less stressful. Remember, the mind is a terrible thing to waste. Once you make your mind up about something then you will be able to do it. As my sister always said, "There is nothing more powerful than a Made Up Mind!" She was right! Everything, and I mean everything, I have set my mind to achieving I have received it. As long as I believed it, it came to past. Actually you can try the Made-Up Mind technique on anything from dieting to exercising to cleaning the house. It really works, not because I said so because He said so. His word says that "anything that we believe in our heart and do not doubt then we shall receive it".

Writing to Affirm Your Beliefs

Also, writing can be useful for keeping track of affirmations that you make with yourself. For instance, you can write a motivating quote or poem and place it on paper and tape it to the refrigerator or your bed post or even on your mirror, anywhere you have to look all the time. If you tell yourself you can then you can and if you tell yourself you can't then you can't. Many years ago in a Psychology 101 course, they taught us that a part of our personality, the ego, has to be right all the time. Its job is to make the truth out of whatever you have in your head. Therefore, if you keep reminding yourself that you are a lousy writer, dancer, singer, worker, mother, wife, friend or anything else, then you will be. The ego's job is to make you right. Likewise if you tell yourself that you are good at these same things, you will be. For sure the ego does not discriminate nor judge, it only acts. So think positive and start writing and affirming your Success!

What should you be writing down? Try these- - of course you can always expand this list with your own thoughts.

1. Past successes
2. Future dreams
3. Things, Thoughts, People and Places to let go of
4. Prayer request
5. Answered prayers
6. Memorable events in your life

In the Space Below Record
Your Future Goal, Vision and Purpose

_____
_____
_____
_____
_____
_____
_____
_____
_____
_____
_____
_____
_____
_____
_____
_____
_____
_____
_____
_____
_____
_____
_____
_____
_____

Chapter 4

Positively Speaking

*"Speech is the mirror of the soul;
as a man speaks, so he is".* **Publilius Syrus**

What is spoken from our mouths demonstrates what we are feeling in our hearts. If we are thinking negative thoughts then our conversations will have a negative tone to it. Most people don't realize why others are always able to see through them, it is because they tell us what they are thinking or feeling by their conversation. It took me a long time to fully understand this principle. Never mind the fact that the Word of God reminds us that we create Life and Death with our tongue. The tongue is referred to as a deadly member of our body. Not enough can be said here about how serious this matter is. For now we will settle with knowing that it is an area that we must forever learn and work on. It is so easy to make slips of the tongue that can have devastating impacts on the lives of others, even on our own lives. How many times have we put our own selves down with our negative self talk or doubting comments?

Words are very powerful and carry with them the ability to bring life or death to a situation. This is serious business and should not be taken lightly. Through words God created the entire universe and everything in and on it. This issue of speaking is so important that there is a whole school of theory and thought on communications, linguistics and language. More than we could adequately cover in such a short period, yet worthy of being mentioned. Most of us speak the way we do because it was how we were spoken to as we were growing and developing. Our speech and conversation have been shaped by our environments and family upbringing. As adults, we have the ability and responsibility to correct anything that we were taught that was incorrect.

No Blame

It's not that we are blaming anyone for what we were taught, for we all love our parents and realize that they did what they were able to do, its just that when you become a man or a woman you now have the ability to make changes to enhance your childhood training and learning. In some cases, you have to start from scratch. Every situation is unique and slightly different.

In my case, I had parents that were highly educated, (though not a formal education) yet I rejected education as a youth. I was very rebellious and did not place any value on education other than what I learned from the streets about getting over and getting by with as little effort as possible. I regret the part I played during that time, but there is no way I can go back. I have accepted my past and have been able to move forward in the positive things of life. Now I have created a habit of Success (not without God's help of course) and He has given me success at everything that I put my hand to, as He promised in Psalms 1.

In order to attain this level of success, you only need to ask for His help and take an active role in changing the way in which you speak to yourself as well as to others. Remember, He is watching to see if we are as faithful to the things that we claim or if we are only pretending. What we say out of our mouths is a good indication of what is in our hearts.

The Pitfalls of Negative Self Talk

Most of us are used to having people share their negative feelings with us on all sorts of topics. Sometimes their comments are a response to something that we have told them about our personal lives. However, the bigger problem is when we start to believe their comments or worst we believe the negative things that we say to ourselves. More often, negative thoughts about ourselves is usually the residue of repeating to ourselves what others have been telling us about ourselves for years. This is a behavior you need to put a stop to immediately. My sister (I have four sisters) once told me something that has stuck with me down through the years, she said "No one's opinion of me matters more than my opinion of myself". This made me realize that their opinions are not valid or something that I have to accept and the positive opinions that I have of me are valid and the ones that I will accept and act upon.

The problem with negative self-talk is that it can go undetected for years and eventually you start to internalize the roles and characteristics that you or someone else has assign to you. Changing this behavior may not come overnight, but if you work at it diligently it will not be impossible to accomplish.

Keep in mind that lasting and true *Change* (as we discussed in chapter one) happens gradually as you make one step at a time and remember to look at your journal (directions from chapter two) from time to time to see how far you have come. Once you get accustomed to your new behaviors they will seem less fearful.

Replacing Negative with Positive Self Talk

Negative self-talk can and does go undetected in most of us most of the time. This is one of the reasons that it is so damaging. The other thing that we are not conscience of is how much negative and damaging things we put out into the universe on a regular basis as it relates to others. There was a time when I spent 90% of my conversations talking about somebody else's problems and issues. All the while mine were growing bigger and more complex day after day and year after year. Now wait, before you come down too hard on me, think back, take that true look at yourself, and see if you had periods in your life where you did the same thing. Oh I know, its hard to look at ourselves and find fault, but that is exactly what this book is designed to do. Part of the process of moving into empowerment is being honest about who we are and changing into who we want to become. Now that is about as plain as I can put it. As my husband would say *"Keep it Real"* .

Now that it has been brought to our attention we have the perfect opportunity to arrest it and delete this bad habit of talking about others. One sure fire way to do this is start paying attention to our thoughts and when we sense that we are going to say something negative, replace our negative comments with a positive one. If you find it difficult to say something positive then try saying nothing at all or just say "watermelon." This is a little trick we were taught in our church choir to say when you didn't remember the words to a song.

Take a look at the following example of what negative talk can do to a person. As we grow and develop, we pick up a sense of who we are and what we can and cannot do or should not do from others. As a matter of fact, if you want to ruin a child for life, continue to tell the child that they can't. Likewise if you want to boost a child's esteem and confidence constantly affirm positive remarks to the things they do and want to be. Even if the child has no intention of being that thing they will still develop a positive outlook on their life because they will have faith in themselves.

My point here is that even though we can not control what is happening to us as we grow up we can make a change once we become adults and there is no excuse for us not to make the necessary adjustments so that we can be as successful as possible.

Again the quickest way to break a habit is to replace it with a new habit. Now would be a good time for developing a new habit of <u>Positive Talk</u>. Tell yourself something good about you each and everyday. Don't worry that you are over doing it, there is no way to over compliment yourself as long as you keep centered on Jesus Christ. Positive self-talk sounds something like this, "I'm good at____; I did a great job by completing _____; It felt good to participate in such and such" or something to this affect.

Try filling in the above blanks with some positive affirmations about your life. Okay, so you know the drill. It will feel awkward at first, but as you do it more and more it will become lest troublesome and before long it will become a habit that you can add to your list of accomplishments. Oh yeah, that list, the one you started several days ago, back when you were reading chapter three, now would be a good time to add to it or even possibly finish it.

The goal is to think before you speak and think before you think. Your speech and thoughts should be in alignment with each other. Think good thoughts so that you will have good things to say.

What you think will guide your actions and what you do will guide your future. Your future holds your success and it all starts with being motivated enough to Live the Empowered Life!

In the Space Below Record
Positive Self Talk or Positive Comments
about those that You know or are close to.

_____

_____

_____

_____

_____

_____

_____

_____

_____

_____

_____

_____

_____

_____

_____

_____

_____

_____

_____

_____

Chapter 5

Making Each Step Solid

"One today is worth two tomorrows; what I am to be, I am now becoming." **Benjamin Franklin**

No matter how dark the road or the way may get if you have someone that is going before you with a light, you will always feel safe and secure knowing that your way is made bright.

This is exactly what it feels like to put our trust in the one and only one who can care for us perfectly and completely. Oh, I know, man is good at helping and assisting God in the things on this earth, but lets face it "when man says no, God says yes", when man can't, God can, when man won't, God will! Who would not serve and depend on "a God like that"?

I have learned to trust in God for every step that I make. As a matter of fact, I can't afford not to trust Him completely. He's just that kind of God. He blesses and cares for us even though we don't deserve it. Even when I am unsure about the step, I have faith in the one who knows all the plans that He has for me and even the plans that He has allowed me to chose for myself. See when you obey and trust your "Father" He will give you what so ever your heart desires. So, let me ask you a question. What is stopping you from doing what you want to make your life happy, peaceful and complete? Think on this for several minutes before reading on. Write your answer to this question on one of the journal pages.

After you have realized that a change needs to happen and you have assessed your past and let go of the things that are holding you down, it should be clear to you that the only thing that is keeping you from your goal and destiny in life is you.

> "I know the plans that I have for
> you they are plans to Prosper you,
> to Give you a hope and a future."

Sounds to me like your creator wants nothing but the best for you. What do you want for you? How much longer will you settle for mediocre instead of abundance and prosperity. Don't delay, take action today. Get with the program. God's program is perfect with no defects. Man will always have some defect in his plan, there is always room for error. This is not so with God. In other words, stop worrying and start living!

This is easier said than done for most people. One reason is that we always think of more reasons (excuses) to not do something. There is always this fear that someone will block or hinder our efforts. That's just it, fear is the major thing that holds us back and eventfully sets us back. I'm here today to tell you that "A Setback is A Setup for A Comeback." I used to hear a motivational speaker, Dr. Robin Eubanks, say that all the time. It just stuck with me. Today, I refuse to let anything hold me back. It may set me back, but it will not keep me back. I have learned how to make each step solid! Once you start doing things right it will make you feel better. The better you feel the more you will be apt to repeat the behavior. If you will just believe and take action on your belief you will see it.

And what we don't release to fear we give in to procrastination which sometimes has as its base, fear. Fear and procrastination go hand in hand. In the absence of fear great things can be accomplished. So it is imperative that you face fear and put it in its proper place, behind you! Remember, fear is something we see when we take our eyes off the prize or the goal. As long as you continue to work toward your goal then you won't have time to fear anything.

Don't be a Victim of Procrastination

There will always be others who are willing, ready and anxious to do what you fail to achieve. Your lack of action is someone's gold mine that could have been yours had you taken the effort to get it done, but no you continued to put it off. Many times we are broke and in need of money yet the very thing that could bring us some income will never happen because of tendencies to procrastinate. I know everyone, once in a while, will procrastinate here and there. But I'm not talking about a little bit here and there. I speaking of severe cases that have caused some of you to lose jobs, homes, apartments and love ones simply because you kept putting off till tomorrow what should and could have been done today.

The reason I know so much about this problem is because I have been faced with my own share of procrastination for years. I can assure you it is not something I intend to go to my grave with. In other words, I have a plan to work on the problem each and every day. I can truly say that I have made great strides, but I still have a ways to go. I know that if you suffer from this problem you are neither hopeless nor helpless. If it can work for me it can work for anybody! You take it one day at a time and continue working on it until all traces of the problem is eliminated. It starts with having faith that God can and will deliver you from the attack of Procrastination. Procrastination is defined as "putting off until tomorrow what you could do today."

The enemy thought he had won when he put me under the attack of procrastination, well he should have killed me when he had the chance, because now I know who I am and *Whose* I am. Therefore, there is nothing that he can do to stop me from reaching my destiny and fulfilling my divine purpose. You must have faith, not just in you, but in the one who created you and created you with a purpose in mind. Therefore, you can achieve what so ever you set your mind to. Just take action and see for yourself. Procrastination is a set up for failure by the enemy.

If you spend time giving yourself reasons for not starting a project you are letting procrastination win. Some people go to their grave without having pursued an idea simply because they were afraid what others thought or did not think. Don't let this happen to you, take the time to live your dreams no matter what you will have to give up to achieve it. You and you alone will be happy in the end. You are capable of achieving great things. The enemy knows this and that is why he is always trying to stop you or place obstacle after obstacle in your path. He is hoping that you will give in so that he can win. You have to just buck up and stay your hand to the mission. I have worked on projects for years before realizing that the hardest work of all was to believe in myself and to keep pushing for the rest. In the end, I have overcome every obstacle and so can you. You're still here aren't you? Well act like it and get busy!

Overcoming Fear and Rejection

If you are going to live the truly empowered life you will have to get over being rejected. There is no room for feelings of sadness, because someone rejected you, for the empowered person.

I used to wonder what was wrong with me, why wasn't I able to do the things that I so longed for in my heart. After several years of wondering, I began to see that I was just plain ole afraid of failure and that kept me from doing a lot of things that I really wanted to do. At first, I thought it was kind of crazy when I heard someone say that "those who don't accomplish great things are just afraid of failing" and because l did not want to face the truth I lead myself down a long dark path that ended in bitterness. I was bitter about everything, my education, my looks, my finances, my career, my love life and my family. I just could not get over the fact that life had dealt me a bad hand.

After going through the stages of bitterness, I began to accept the way I was and I decided to make a change. I had actually hit my "rock-bottom", a phrase you hear when alcoholics refer to when talking about a colleague that has to hit rock-bottom before they can get help and make a change. Well I was no alcoholic, but I still had to hit this "rock bottom" to fear and rejection before I could obtain "good success".

Well, after I faced the truth about my being afraid of failure, I was able to get help. I spent almost every waking moment reading self-help books. Everything from Dr. Wayne Dwyer to Les Brown and all the other noted and non-noted motivational and inspirational speakers, including the Bible. (then I realized that I had the number one self help book in my possession all my life) What I discovered very rapidly is that they all had a central theme for getting on with your life and being prosperous.

It all starts with the individual making choices and taking action to support the choice. What a brainstorm. I started believing what I was reading and hearing and before long I was fully motivated to reach the success I had only dreamed of as a child. There are things that I have done in my life that I never dreamed possible for me to do in my life time and be able to share it with others. It is simply unbelievable. You too can begin to live your dreams by making the first step.

Start small, set little daily goals for yourself and keep track of your accomplishments. As you reach each goal treat yourself to something special to reaffirm your achievement. This will boost your moral and give you a reason to try something even bigger. Never, ever, ever forget to give all praises to whom they are due. If you forget this piece you may as well be dead. I feel like Paul when he said, all that I have and have accomplished is like dung compared to knowing Jesus Christ and following Him.

Blessings Come in Small and Large Packages

It is an honor and a blessing that He allows you and me to enjoy the fruits of our labor. Always look for little or big ways to participate in your own life's successes. When you take an active role the better you will feel about yourself. Remember, as you grow, so grows your challenges. The bigger the challenge the larger the success. Keep in mind that you were born for success! You were destine for greatness!

In the space below start to make a small list of the things that you wish to accomplish this year. Try to think of the things as if money or race is of no object. What ever you do and where ever you go, Make Each Step Solid. You never know when you will need to travel that road again.

Come on, this is your chance to *Release Your Power*!

RELEASE YOUR POWER

In the Space Below Record Things You want to Achieve in the next Year.

_____

_____

_____

_____

_____

_____

_____

_____

_____

_____

_____

_____

_____

_____

_____

_____

_____

_____

_____

Chapter 6

Building Solid Relationships

"How shall two walk together unless they agree"

In order to get from here to there you must be able to count on the help of one another. Without this natural need to be together in close relationship, we would not have been able to replenish the earth, have no means to learn how we are to be in relationship with our heavenly Father nor survive in communities as the population continued to grow. In anything that we do we must rely on the help and assistance of others. Think about this for a minute, where would we live without the assistance of others. Consider our shelter, food and medical needs. How far could you get if you had to build your own house? What if you had to kill your own bull just to eat a steak? I certainly would not know how to make a bar of soap let alone treat myself for any serious medical issue. Lets face it, we would not get very far in life if we could not depend on others.

Most people live in either an apartment or house, or some dwelling that was built by others and even if you built it yourself, you probably got the materials from someone else. It probably took at least 3 to 4 people to complete the simplest home. When we eat, we have to depend on the fact that someone else made, killed and / or prepared the food.

And when was the last time that you had to depend on others for such things as medical care or advice, education, learning or training? What about your children, who do you turn to when you need a break from the children or if you are a working parent, who is assisting you with daycare? This is just a small sample of how much we depend on each other. Whether we like it or not we are all interconnected and made interdependent on each other. Therefore, it seems to me that it is extremely important that we take heed to how we are treating each other.

The relationships that we form or build are as important as we are to ourselves. There are many, right now, waiting on someone to come through with a kidney or heart so that they might live longer and healthier lives. Yes, there is absolutely no way that we can get around this thing of depending on others and we should strive to treat each other with a lot more love and respect then we are currently doing.

Helping Others Helps You

What does it mean to treat others in a way that we are helping not only them but helping ourselves? It means going to a higher level in humanity. A level that is reserved for those who want more out of life then just merely surviving. Life is highly mysterious and no man (or woman) has been able to find the answers to all that is at the center of our beings. The Bible tells us that "God's ways and thoughts are much higher than ours, as high as the heavens are from the earth, is as high as His ways are from ours". This very truth says a great deal. One thing we do know is that we are all connected one way or the other. The more you help others the more help you receive. We reap what we sow. What you give out is what you get back. Sometimes it is returned to you in greater measure. If you mistreat someone a little bit, you may get mistreatment back in a greater measure in some other area of your life. Be careful of how you treat those that are in relationship with you. We should be building people up not tearing them down. What kind of person enjoys tearing others down? What ever kind they are, I always try to stay away from these kinds of people. It was not always like that for me.

I use to always hang around people that were tearing me down or putting me down. But that was in the days when I did not know very much. I did not feel good about myself in those days. Today I am different. I am in the same body but my heart and mind is different. I think and act different. It seemed that I was always giving and not getting much in returned. Then one day God turned it all around and people just started coming out of the woodwork and started pouring into my life.

I asked God why all this was happening to me. It wasn't that I was ungrateful, I just wanted to know. I knew I did not do anything to deserve all that people were doing for me. That's when God showed me that all that time that people called me stupid and a fool for what I did for others, God was pleased and it is His good pleasure to give us the kingdom. Blessed are the lowly, meek and the poor. They will inherit much. I was only receiving what had been prepared in my inheritance. Many complain and criticize and God blesses.

Don't waste time fighting it just do it. It follows the

spiritual truths of "the more you give the more you receive". What you give out is what you get back. If you sow seeds of doubt and dislike then you will reap the same things. If you sow seeds of optimism and faith then you will bring these things into your own life. You and you alone have the choice as to how you will treat others so it is up to you as to how high you will go as an individual. Most people get so caught up in trying to pay others back that they miss the mark of rising to a higher level of humanity. They don't value relations and end up being very bitter, angry and jealous when they see others elevated or promoted or just being joyful. It's a shame when people dislike you or can't stand you because you are in a good mood or joyful all the time. They actually don't believe that it can happen. It can. Try it!

To Burn or Not to Burn

How many times have you heard someone say "don't burn your bridges." They say this because they believe that at some point in your life's journey you may have to come back over a path that you have crossed before and you don't want anything to hinder your future. It is a warning statement about the way in which we leave a relationship or situation. I have had that happen to me where I mistreated someone and ended up needing that person again and there were ill feelings. This might cause the person that would otherwise help to refuse to help. This is a good reason to not burn your bridges. On the other hand, there are times when we need to not only burn the bridge but to "blow it up!"

If you are wise you will not burn the bridges that you may have to travel again. However, there are some bridges that need to be burned. Immediately!

For instance, I needed to burn the bridge of prostitution. This was not a path that I wanted to cross again. I needed to burn the bridge of procrastination, illegal drug use and abuse and infidelity. Often times people just stick with the "don't burn any bridges" concept and this leaves them in the vulnerable position of going back to some places that they never need to visit again. So, there are times when we do need to burn a few bridges. But this is not the case all of the time. There are many times when we will be put in the same situation and we may depend on the person that we came across in the past. Therefore, we should seek to build positive relationships. Never mind the fact He told us to "love everybody even those that hate and abuse us."

Throughout this life, we do not know where we will go and where we will end up. This is why it is important to treat people along the way the manner in which we ourselves want to be treated. I know that me personally, I want to be treated with respect and love. I expect to be loved because God said to love others. If I give out love then I expect to reap love. He did say that we shall reap what we sow.

Even if I don't get the love from the same place that I sowed it does not mean it won't come. If I sow love and no one on earth loves me back I am still way ahead of the game because I know that God always loves me.

Often we think that it is okay to treat people the way others have treated us or maybe we just like hurting others, but what we don't realize is that since we are all connected at some point and time it will come back to haunt you. I know that it is tempting and very hard to resist getting back at others, but resist is what you have to do if you are going to live a victorious life where you experience success after success. You simply must make up your mind to treat each person that you come into contact with as someone that you may have to depend on at a later date.

By doing this, you are releasing a positive energy into your life that will prosper and give off the same energy and bring you happiness, power and success at all you set your hand to.

Practice Self Control

I was once told by a black belt karate expert that when we get angry and display it, it is the same as losing self-control. He further shared with me that losing control of our emotions to the point that we are yelling and scream-ing is the lowest form of humanity. I was almost off my chair as I listened to this person talk about something that I had never heard or considered in my entire life.

To think that for years we have been going around in this lower state of humanity by losing our "cool". From that point on I made up my mind to be very careful about getting and displaying my anger. Prior to talking with him I was not concerned with how or when I displayed anger or lost "my cool" so to speak. But when you stop to think about it what reason do we have for "going off on people?"

What does it solve?" When you really stop to think about it, it only makes you look bad. People actually become physically unattractive when they are in an outrage or state of anger. Their entire appearance changes. Just like your appearance changes when you are in a good mood. You know, that look when people seem to be "glowing."

The sad thing is that most people believe that they cannot control their emotions. I suggest to those who might feel that way to take one step at a time and learn all you can about the subject of self-control. If you have to enroll in a karate course, then by all means do so. Self empowerment includes being self-controlled. You control yourself by allowing the spirit to control you. Besides, how successful can you really feel if you are always "losing your cool." It could cost you one of those bridges.

Because we have these great minds and are able to have wisdom, then we should be able to exercise control over our actions, remember as we stated earlier, its not as important what happens to us but rather it is our reaction to what happens that causes all of us the problems. I am sure that if you are like me then you are able to think on many occasions where you got upset and displayed anger and then later wish you had not acted in the manner in which you did.

Since we are still on earth then we are still in a position to improve and make the changes for a better you. Don't waste another minute. Start living the empowered life today!

In the Space Below Record
A List of Relationships that You want to cultivate or strengthen and Why.

_____

_____

_____

_____

_____

_____

_____

_____

_____

_____

_____

_____

_____

_____

_____

_____

_____

_____

_____

_____

_____

_____

_____

Chapter 7

Developing The Leader Within

"Real leaders are ordinary people with extraordinary determinations." **John Seaman Garns**

Growing up I never felt much like a leader. I was told by many people in society that I was a follower. I believed what people told me and soon started acting like a follower. I would follow people because I wanted to feel as though I "fit in." I just never thought of myself as a leader. In January of 1980, I ended up in the United States Navy by following behind my younger sister Beverly.

My sister suggested that we go into the military on the "buddy system." She had been to speaking with a recruiter and she assured me that we would always be together. I was so excited about doing something positive that I would have followed her anywhere. This offer to go in the military came at a time in my life when I was not doing anything. Just hanging out with people that were going nowhere fast. Going into the military with my sister was an answered prayer. I was finally going to do something worth while. I was going to make my mother proud of me.

My sister, Cookie, and I had always done everything together and we were so close. After being sworn in, my sister informed me that she was not going to join. I was devastated! There was nothing I could do. I was already sworn in to the Navy and was scheduled to be shipped off to boot camp on January 2, 1980. After overcoming the initial shock, I set my mind to have a good time. I learned a lot about motivation and leadership in the military.

While in Boot Camp, one of our first assignments was to answer the question, "what is a leader?" I never forgot that question or my response and what happened as a result of my response. I simply said, "a leader is someone that has to first be a good follower". I believe that I responded that way due to the fact that I had been told that I was a follower and I was searching for something inside of me to justify that what I was would one day lead to something good. It did. Today, I am told by many that I am a leader. However, I have learned to not put too much stock in what people tell you. After all they were wrong before. That is why I believe that you have to know you for yourself and know who God says that you are.

As a result of that response, I was one of five women selected from our 80 member squad that was chosen to be a Section Leader during our 8 weeks of basic training. My mother was very proud of me because she stills remembers that until this day. There's just one little problem. No one had ever taught me how to be a leader and I failed to pick it up along with all the junk that I pick up in my life experiences.

Instead of picking up on the latest songs, outfits, entertainment, and drugs, I should have been reading books on the life and times of great leaders and studying which leadership skills are most important for success. Though I had been chosen for a leadership role, I failed the first time at bat because I did not have the tools to sustain my position. I did not even have enough sense to watch the other 4 leaders to see how they were handling their roles. This can be a terrible thing. It is bad enough that you don't know how to do something. But it is even worse to not know that you can learn just about anything from watching others. Now this is not to say that everyone is to be what you see others being or doing. I am talking about the same thing that happens when you watch someone wash windows and now you can do it. My point is that we can learn a lot more than we give ourselves credit for. Don't give up before you try!

Today, I am committed to helping young people develop the concept of being a leader in every area of their lives regardless of their background. I work with inner city youth. I wonder how many of them thought like I did when I was their age. At 12 and 13 years old, I did not think about anything but what was the latest dance, song and outfit. I never wondered about my education level. We have to prepare the youth that we are around. No one knows where their life will take them and when they will be called upon to be a leader. There is a quote that says,

"Its better to have and not need
than to need and not have."

Born Great

You must embrace the mind set that every person has the potential to be *GREAT!* You were made by a Great God and made in His image. You were fearfully and wonderfully made. Therefore, you were born to be great. Your job is to live out this greatness in this life time. As soon as you do this the world will receive your gift. If you thought that you were left out you are wrong! God has shown me this through my own life and has raised me up to teach this truth to others.

When I was in the 9th grade I had an Algebra teacher write on one of my test papers "you have potential." During those days I used to get *"high"* before school, during school and after school. I went to a school where students did what they wanted. We even smoked marijuana on the school grounds. However, this teacher noticed something about Lilisa's work. I can't remember him ever telling me face to face anything that would spark a liking to school or cause me to change my bad habits. But on my paper he wrote those words. At the time I did not know what the word "potential" meant, all I know is that I liked the sound of it.

It wasn't until I was grown that I understood the meaning of the word. All I can say now is that he was right. It didn't do me much good in those days since I did not know the meaning of the word but today I live the *Empowered* life because I realize that I have the potential for greatness. So no matter who you are and where you've been you too have the *Potential* to be great and live a truly Empowered Life!

Now I understand why so many people feel as though they do not have great potential. It all stems from some of the concepts in the first six chapters of this book. More than likely there was some one that told you - - - you were not great or made you feel as though you were not great.

However, they do not know you for real so you have every right to live out the greatness that God put inside of you before you were born. If I had continued living under clouds of deceptions I had developed for myself over the years, I would not be where I am today. I would not be a recent graduate from an accredited MBA program, I would not be an author of two books and working on a third. I would not be married to a handsome man that does not abuse me but loves the Lord and loves me the way Christ loves the Church. No, the way my life started I did not believe I would one day be doing the things that I am doing these days. What I know today is that if God did it for me He will do it for you too! I believe I have the power today to lead and that I had it with me all the time.

The Leader Within

Being a leader is not just about telling other people what to do. It is also about telling yourself what to do! It is about honing your leadership skills so that you will be able to fulfill the perfect will of God for your life.

Leadership skills are needed for almost every area of life. If you are on the job you need leadership skills to help your department or organization meet its goals and objectives. If you are a family member then you certainly need leadership skills to help your spouse and / or children or siblings reach their goals and purpose in life. If you are in the church you most definitely need leadership skills. You need them to help your church fulfill its God ordained mission.

As a leader, you have to take authority over your life and cancel every wicked thing that has ever been spoken over your life and start speaking the blessings that were spoken over your life by God through His son, Jesus Christ.

There are many examples that we could give of great leaders. For instance, Dr. Martin Luther King, Jr. was a great leader. He lead our country through a tough period of injustices and oppressions against blacks. Today we are enjoying the fruits of his labor. Moses of the Old Testament led millions out of oppression, poverty and death into a land that flowed with milk and honey. An interesting point about both of these leaders is that they did not live to see the new place that they fought hard to lead the people into. This is the sign of a truly great leader, leading even if you don't get to see the thing that you fought for. Both of these leaders where great men of faith. They were willing to sacrifice their life for the success of others.

If you are truly going to be a great leader and live the empowered life you have to live by your faith. Jesus Christ was and is the greatest leader of all because He gave His life for those that were against Him. Jesus gave up His life for those that did not know, love or like Him, as a matter of fact He even gave it for those that hate Him. This clearly makes Him the greatest of them all!

Leadership Skills at Work

There is not enough leadership skills demonstrated in most work places. Some leaders think that leadership skills are for only a select few. They do not grasp the fact that if leadership skills are developed in the people that work around them that the company or team will grow much faster and to a greater degree.

The development of leaders within an organization is the single most important task that senior management faces. When an organization has great leaders, with excellent leadership skills and qualities, in place, superior performance is seen at every level of the business. Leadership development helps organizations to determine what they want from the market, the workforce and the industry. Good leadership not only allows managers to determine the desired course but it is through their efforts, in coordinating and aligning team and mission, that getting there is accomplished. On the other hand, without good leadership the organization will often find itself in a state of chaos which could lead to poor performance and failure.

Organizations need leaders at all stages. They need seasoned leaders to set the vision. They need emerging leaders to come up with new ideas. They need senior leaders to remind them of the mission and to research the success of other companies and keep senior leaders informed about other environmental factors.

Leaders are important to a company because they are able to see the vision and move the workforce to take on new challenges and develop new products and services that will support their business goals and objectives. Companies must get on board with developing their leaders or they will find themselves swallowed up by other companies or find themselves extinct due to the inability to adapt with the changing environments.

There will always be a gap between what is done and what should be done because people are in different places at different stages. This is precisely the reasons for having strong leadership because it is the leader that can see the vision, make the adjustments and pull the rest of the people into the fold.

Why all the talk about leaders and leadership? In my research on the state of leaders within organizations, I found that there is a lot of talk about a future leadership problem. My research included reading books by Robert Slater, "Jack Welch and the GE Way," John C. Maxwell, "Developing the Leaders Around You," and Hans Finzel, "The Top Ten Mistakes Leaders Make," and a number of scholarly research articles. These writers fear a loss of properly prepared leadership in the future.

Research conducted by Development Dimensions International (DDI), a global workforce and leadership training, staffing and assessment firm, predict a 40% - 50% gap in available leaders and the need for leaders, over the next five years. If this trend continues, it will leave most major and older companies grasping for qualified leaders to fill their top positions and not enough qualified replacements.

This gap will continue to cause a problem as many employees that would make great candidates for leadership are often looked over for a number of reasons, one being that they are not part of the political circle. This is very unfortunate for the employee and the company. In the end, these individuals may leave and go to a firm where their talents can be developed and utilized. The company that did not recognize the value of good leadership potential is the real loser.

The other side of this scenario is when the employee, though they feel an inner pull to lead and/or develop their leadership potential, do not realize his or her own talent and they end up staying with the company for many years, without any real development. Then one day, several years later, they read a success story about a person who reminds them of themselves and realizes that they could have reached success had they listened to their inner most feelings. Usually by this time, they are close to or ready for retirement. What a tragic lost of life! But this is the sort of thing that happens every day in the business world.

Don't let this happen to you. Start living out your purpose in life and take the time to assess your skills and talents and learn how to develop those areas that may be lacking. Take charge of your life and your career. You were born with some talent or many talents. It is up to you to hone in on those talents and look for ways and opportunities to develop them. More than likely, the opportunities are right under your nose. You will need power to stand against all the "nay Sayers" who will tell you "you can't do it." Empowered people press forward anyway!

Be a Leader that Empowers Others

An effective leader helps others find their purpose in life, in career, and at home. This is because a great leader knows his/her own purpose. Therefore, they have the skills, talents and abilities to help others with self-development. A great leader is not afraid to help others reach higher heights. Leading people in the right direction will cause you, the leader, to grow! Your growth will spill onto everyone around you. This will expand your operation, regardless of where you are, whether at home, at church or in the business world. Your territory will increase. As others see that you really care about them thy will be willing to follow and help you achieve great things. This principle is often practiced by the leaders of gangs and/ or the Mafia.

It just makes good sense to build up the people around you. After all, why would you want people around you who are so weak and depressed due to your lack of empowerment or belief in them. If one tears the people down around them what kind of help will they really be able to get from this? None! It does not take a "rocket scientist" to figure this out! You don't have to take my words for it— - - - if you are any kind of a leader, just try it and let me know if it works for you. No doubt—it will!!

Remember, you are a leader. If nothing else you are "A Leader of One." You always will be responsible for leading yourself. After all, outside of God and the Holy Spirit, who else would you want to give that task over too.

You have to tell and convince yourself that you are more than a conqueror through Him that loves you. And if any battle gets to big just know that the battle is not yours anyway. The battle *is* the Lord's! Stop fighting and start Releasing Your Power!

If you don't do what you are purposed to do then who will do it? The very moment you begin walking in your purpose you will EXPLODE!!! No matter how old or how young you are it is never too late or too early to do and be the things that you were created to do and be.

Go on, develop the leader within!

In the Space Below Record
A List of the Leadership Skills that you already possess and those you want to cultivate.

_____

_____

_____

_____

_____

_____

_____

_____

_____

_____

_____

_____

_____

_____

_____

_____

_____

_____

_____

_____

_____

_____

_____

Chapter 8

Continuous Improvement

"In the business of life, Man is the only product. And there is only one direction in which man can possibly develop if he is to make a better living or yield a bigger dividend to himself, to his race, to nature or to God. He must grow in knowledge, wisdom, kindliness and understanding."
V.C. Kitchen

In business, a product or service undergoes an improvement process for the life of that product or service. In life, you must continue to improve your product and service....*self.* Throughout life you are "growing or slowing." To keep up with life you must add to yourself so that you live a productive life.

Just like little children who are constantly redefining themselves through their experiences and their trials, so we must adopt this childlike behavior if we are going to reach our full potential. Remember, life is a process. It is a series of experiences that shape and define who and what we are.

If at any point and time we feel that we have chosen the wrong responses to life then we need to re-group, re-assess and make changes that will put us closer to our desired goals. Don't just settle for what you see on the surface. Continue the process of improvement with each new day of your life. This is what makes life exciting.   W   e should always look deep inside of ourselves for areas that have not been transformed (made over) yet.

If you are like me you have had a few knocks and hits by life, don't let it destroy your spirit. Never let a knock down become a knock out. Continue to hope for better times, knowing that they could be just a day away. Les Brown, the renowned motivational speaker, used to say, "If I can look up then I can get up". Sometimes life has to knock some sense into us. Sometimes life will throw you a lemon and you need to know how to make lemonade. You will never know what is actually on the inside of you until you have been squeezed. Situations in life provide the squeezing.   If life throws you something that you don't want, simply throw it back. If your future shows you a picture you don't want to see, draw a new picture. As you add to your knowledge you are changing who you are.

Since we are made in the image of our creator, we are all individual images of a creator and therefore, fully capable of re-creating ourselves. We are better at this process when we get the help of our original creator and He purposes it in the hearts of others to help us. We learned in the chapter on building solid relationships that we are all connected.

If you continue to practice the steps in this book, you will have success- - -continually! I started this journey (life) being a victim of child sexual abuse. I dropped out— —

no flunked out of high school with an 8th grade education. I spent most of my teenage years partying. I had no clue about what I wanted to do in my future. I thought that one day I would just wake up and be successful. I did not know that I had to work at it. I did not know how to work at it. I thought success, as I saw it on T.V., was for others, not for me. Without having followed the steps in this book I do not know where my life would be today.

Practicing the principles in this book, along with others that you have collected along your journey will keep you busy until all your processing is complete. Don't worry you have more than enough time for all this. The process will only end when you reach the end of your life! The key is to never give up trying new things to add to your success. As long as you are here, you have the grand opportunity to work your plan and use your life as a canvas to paint a picture of what you want your life to look like. Until death, you have the ability to create your new ending. Take advantage of your time.

Some people never live the empowered successful life because they get stuck in a rut and fail to see how they should move forward. They see failure as the end as opposed to looking for a new way to try their dream. Others don't feel that their life is as important as someone like, say Michael Jackson or Shaqueal O'Neal but let me reassure you, that according to our heavenly Father, we are all created with a specific purpose and it is up to us to find out just what that purpose is. Don't waste time trying to be like anyone else. Just be the best you can be. My life went to a whole new level and took on new meaning when I gave up putting myself down for what I did not have and started celebrating myself for what I did have. I discovered that I had many hidden talents that I had never considered. When I was working as a janitor, presser (dry cleaning), or a jet mechanic I did not know that I would one day be an entrepreneur, college professor, preacher and

and author. I never saw myself as an executive or leader. Now that I have overcome my past, setbacks and pitfalls, I can truly say that what happens to us is not nearly as important as how we react to what has happened. I used to say why me Lord? Now I say why not me? I say, why not you? My success, like any success, did not come easy nor did it come overnight. It took years of hard work, sacrifice and study.

Preparing for Your Purpose

Finding one's divine purpose in life is the secret to continuous improvement and living the truly empowered life. This is the single most important task before you. If you are on mission to live out your true purpose then you will willingly make the necessary adjustments to yourself that will make you ready to receive your life's purpose at the appointed time. What I have discovered throughout my life is that no matter how much I wanted something or wished that something would go this way or that, it never went the way that made me feel complete and whole until I yielded to my ultimate purpose.

Preparing for your purpose will equip you to live it when the season comes. Failing to prepare will leave you feeling like a failure when opportunity does arrive. You have to prepare for success. If you are prepared when you find your true purpose things just seem to fall into place with little or no effort from you. This purpose has a timing and some things come into our lives to simply teach us how to be patient so that we can reap our harvest in due season. The Bible tells us to wait and to run the race with patience. Until your purpose shows up there are many things that you should be doing. Going to school, saving and investing your money, building solid relationships, journaling, and working out. Just to name a few. You will probably have many more things that you can think of doing while you are searching for your divine purpose in life.

Take this time to prepare your heart, mind, body and emotions for what's in store for you. Spend time assessing your personal talents, likes and dislikes, natural skills and ability. When the proper season comes you do not want to miss out because you are not prepared to handle the size of the harvest. This is what happens to a lot of people, the harvest has been prepared for them but they are unable to benefit because they did not prepare themselves during the time that the harvest was developing. It's as if they could not see what was growing so they were slacking during the time they should have been sharpening the ax.

Most peoples lives are like a roller coaster, a series of ups and downs. Down one day and up the next. One setback after another. This type of living is very frustrating and draining. It can only be changed if you are willing to make small changes now until they become big habits in your life. If you keep plugging away, soon you will be ready for your success. The harvest is already being prepared for you.

I have been sowing (working hard) at continuous improvement for the past 19 years and now I am starting to reap from a harvest that I did not grow. I can do this because I am prepared, I have the right tools and this is the right time- - - to *RELEASE MY POWER!* You can do it too! I am compelled to teach this message to everyone that will listen!

Wake up each and every day and say to yourself, "I will be motivated and positive about what the future holds for me" You will notice your life changing as soon as you make the first change from the old to the new. All you have to do is keep learning and growing; take every opportunity to meet new people; take every opportunity to travel to new places see new and different things. It will open doors that "no man can shut!"

Listen To Your Inner Voice

There is a voice inside each of us that is trying to guide our success. He will lead you to the right school, college, husband/wife, organization, business investment and areas you need to work on. You will have to listen closely and clearly to hear Him speak. Trust this voice. If you knew where to look and what to do you would not be reading this book. He will guide you the right preparation that you will need for you to harvest your fields of success.

Remember:

1. make small changes that are lasting
2. assess your skills and talents
3. keep writing in that journal,
4. stop the practice of negative talk
5. make each step solid
6. surround yourself with positive people
7. hone your leadership potential
8. continue improving everyday

If you do these things on a daily basis you will have the success you want to achieve, accomplish and attain. Before you know it, you will "become who you really are" and able to write your book on how to *"Release Your Power!"*

Begin Recording New Things that You Would like to do or new talents you would like to develop.
"remember, anything is possible"

_____

_____

_____

_____

_____

_____

_____

_____

_____

_____

_____

_____

_____

_____

_____

_____

_____

_____

_____

_____

APPENDIX

Throughout this book, you marked some tips, thoughts, or statements that you may always want to keep. To make them more accessible, go back through the book and find the things you want to remember. Write your favorites in the spaces below or in a journal or notebook. Put the page number of where the tip, thought, or statement in the page box, so you can refer to it quickly. Review you list often.

Page

Page

notes

notes

To Purchase Copies of this book contact us at:

Performance Strategies Unlimited, Inc.
PO Box 5853
Hillside, NJ 07205

Or email us at
info@performancestrategiesunlimited.nct
www.performancestrategiesunlimited.net

For Booking Engagements Contact:

Lilisa J. Williams
Performance Strategies Unlimited, Inc.
PO Box 5853
Hillside, NJ 07205
908-432-1853
info@performancestrategiesunlimited.net
www.performancestrategiesunlimited.net

Author's Bio

Lilisa J. Williams currently resides in Hillside, New Jersey by way of Cincinnati, Ohio, with her husband of Newark, NJ. Her career life journey started in 1980, when she enlisted in the US Navy where she was trained and work as an Aviation Jet Mechanic.

In 1990 she began her academic journey when she enrolled in Essex County College in Newark, New Jersey. She graduated with high honors from Union County College in 1994. After receiving a scholarship for her academic and leadership success she transferred to Fairleigh Dickinson University where she earned a degree in Political Science in 1997. In 1998 she returned to FDU and completed their prestigious MBA program. She is currently pursuing a Ph.D., in Training and Performance Improvement at Capella University.

Lilisa serves as keynote speaker and/or seminar presenter for a variety of organizations throughout the state on New Jersey. She has also been invited to speak in Texas, Ohio and Massachusetts.

She is the founder and president of Performance Strategies Unlimited, Inc. A Motivational , Leadership and Empowerment Training Institute. She is also the author of: God's Plan for My Success "A Personal Testimony About Overcoming the Enemy's Plan to Destroy My Life".

Lilisa's desire is to help others find their way to releasing what God has put down on the inside of them. She attributes much of her success to the things that others have taught her. But, once you are taught,- - - - it is you- - - that must go and do!

Upcoming Books by this Author:

Power of an Effective Leader

Power of Standing Firm

Power of Winning